9600 3178 $15.29

W9-APF-015

PEOPLE POWER

SUSAN
NEIBURG
TERKEL

PEOPLE POWER

A Look at Nonviolent Action and Defense

LODESTAR BOOKS
DUTTON   NEW YORK

ACKNOWLEDGMENTS

I want to thank the numerous people who helped me: my
editor, Rosemary Brosnan; Roger S. Powers and Christopher
Kruegler of the Albert Einstein Institution; Doug Rand of the
Resource Center for Nonviolence; Ruth Benn and Joanne
Sheehan of the War Resisters League; longtime activists
Juanita Nelson, Hattie Nestel, Leo Schiff, and Ken West;
and my colleagues and friends, Pat Jenkins and Jim Wilkens.

Library of Congress Cataloging-in-Publication Data

Terkel, Susan Neiburg.
    People power: a look at nonviolent action and defense/Susan
Neiburg Terkel.
        p.   cm.
    Includes bibliographical references and index.
    Summary: Covers the definition, principles, and methods
of nonviolence, including civil disobedience.
    ISBN 0-525-67434-9 (alk. paper)
    1. Nonviolence—Juvenile literature.   2. Nonviolence—United
States—Juvenile literature.   3. Civil disobedience—Juvenile
literature.   4. Social action—Juvenile literature.
[1. Nonviolence.   2. Civil disobedience.   3. Social action.]
I. Title.
HM278.T375   1996
303.6′1—dc20   95-43578   CIP   AC

Published in the United States by Lodestar Books,
an affiliate of Dutton Children's Books,
a division of Penguin Books USA Inc.,
375 Hudson Street, New York, New York 10014

Published simultaneously in Canada
by McClelland & Stewart, Toronto

Editor: Rosemary Brosnan   Designer: Barbara Powderly
Printed in the U.S.A.   First Edition   10 9 8 7 6 5 4 3 2 1

Contents

vi

Contents

1

The Meaning
of Nonviolence

1

Taking on
Goliath

We have more power than we know.
—David Dellinger

*Never doubt that a small group of thoughtful,
committed citizens can change the world; indeed, it's the
only thing that ever has.*
—Margaret Mead

When Dexter Cate arrived at the Izu Peninsula, some 120 miles southwest of Tokyo, Japan, he was quite unprepared for the sight at the harbor: hundreds of dolphins trapped in a fishing net, swimming frantically through blood-stained water. From a boat nearby, a Japanese fisherman speared one of the dolphins, knowing that if one was wounded, all would panic and none would escape. Dolphins never abandon a wounded member of their group.

Then Cate witnessed dolphins being dragged ashore by their tails. As they thrashed about on the sand and whistled in pain, other fishermen slit open the dolphins' bellies and throats and left the guts hanging out of dolphins that were fighting for their lives. A fisherman sliced the heart out of a dolphin that was still alive and casually threw the heart aside.

After the dolphins died, their bodies were put through a mincing machine and made into fertilizer and pig feed.

A year later, Cate returned to Japan, only to learn that the Japanese government was promoting the mass slaughter of dolphins by offering a bounty of eighty dollars per head. Angered, Cate decided to act.

Just before dawn one day Cate paddled a dinghy out to a small islet in the bay off Iki Island, where Japanese fishermen had trapped approximately three hundred dolphins in nets. Cate set the dolphins free, knowing that his action could cost him his own freedom for a while.

A Japanese court charged Cate with criminal damage. After holding him in jail for three months, the judge gave him a suspended six-month sentence and deported him to Hawaii, where Cate lived.

Soon others followed Cate's lead. After Patrick Wall observed the brutal treatment of dolphins he, too, took action, releasing 150 dolphins before dawn one day. In fact, for years people who were concerned about the fate of dolphins lobbied for laws to protect them—and, like Cate and Wall, defied the law in order to save them. Largely spearheaded by the environmental action group Greenpeace, a grassroots movement to protect the dolphins gained momentum.

The movement to protect the dolphins depended solely on a unique way of fighting—nonviolent action. One by one, people joined the protest, until there were thousands of protesters. A few, like Cate and Wall, carried out direct actions that rescued dolphins. Others banded together to use economic, social, and political power to pressure governments and fishing companies to stop the merciless killing of this precious species.

This book is about nonviolent action—what it is, how it works, and why it is so special.

Power. People power. Nonviolent action is the power of people to fight or resist attack *without using violence.*

Nonviolent action is economic power. When large numbers of people band together and refuse to go to work, or agree to slow down production, they can gain the power to increase their pay and improve their working conditions and benefits. When consumers unite in their refusal to buy certain products or services, they, too, wield economic power.

In their small
inflatable boat,
Greenpeace
volunteers protest
the killing of a
minke whale calf
by Japanese
fishermen.
GREENPEACE/
CULLEY

Poverty and lack of sanitation can make infant formula a deadly alternative to breastfeeding. Yet in its quest for profits, Nestle, an international corporation, encouraged and even pressured mothers in Africa to use infant formula. To protest that policy and to pressure Nestle to change, INFACT, a Boston-based action group, mounted a worldwide campaign against Nestle that cost the company so much in lost revenues and tarnished public image that Nestle agreed to change its policy.[1]

Nonviolent action is political power. If large numbers of citizens protest a government, defy its laws, or set up parallel institutions of their own, they can sometimes successfully transfer power to themselves. Using nonviolent sanctions, Philippine citizens overthrew their

Through its worldwide boycott of Nestle's products, INFACT, of Boston, compelled Nestle to change its marketing policies in developing nations.
INFACT, OF BOSTON

corrupt dictator, Ferdinand Marcos, while citizens of Poland and the former Czechoslovakia, East Germany, and the Soviet Union replaced their Communist parties with prodemocratic governments. "More has been done by nonviolent struggle to liberate people from Communist dictatorship," claims Gene Sharp, a scholar of nonviolent conflict, "than anything the Pentagon has done with all the billions and billions of dollars for forty years."[2]

Some political experts believe that an entire populace can learn to do a wide array of nonviolent sanctions and develop a well-orchestrated plan to use them. In fact, these experts believe that ordinary citizens can actually replace military forces and protect their nation against foreign aggression and attempted takeovers, and even deter a nuclear attack.

Nonviolent action is psychological power. Sometimes, by surprising a would-be assailant with kindness or fearlessness, by using wit or compassion, people can have the power to confuse assailants and thwart an attack. When an escaped inmate from a nearby prison thrust a gun in the face of Louise Degrafinried and her husband, Nathan, the seventy-three-year-old grandmother refused to be bullied into submission.[3]

"Young man," she demanded, "I don't believe in no violence. Put that gun down and you sit down. I don't allow no violence here."

With that admonishment, the escaped convict gingerly placed his gun on her couch. "Lady," he pleaded in a soft voice, "I'm so hungry. I haven't had nothing to eat for three days."

Louise cooked him a hearty breakfast of bacon, eggs, toast, milk, and coffee while Nathan set the kitchen table with their best napkins. When the three sat down to eat, she took the convict's hand and prayed for him. By the time the threesome had finished their meal, and she had prayed for her uninvited guest some more, the police arrived and arrested him—without anyone getting hurt or killed.

Belonging to a group that shares the same vision of success gives people psychological power. When Verna Spaethe's local disabilities-activist group expanded from six members to one hundred in less than a year, the group's morale and determination also grew. "The bond between my sisters and brothers with disabilities transcends all things which might otherwise divide us," Spaethe explains. "We are African-Americans, we are European-Americans; we are women, we are men, we are straight, we are gay; we are rich, we are poor; we are athletes and intellectuals and fun and serious and we share a common vision. We are stronger for this vision . . . we are powerful."[4]

Nonviolent action is social power. Through demonstrations, marches, and a host of creative tactics, groups gain the power to air their grievances and can cause the winds of public opinion to stir in their direction. Each side of the abortion issue, for example, uses social power to argue its case in the public forum.

People can direct the power of nonviolent action toward just about any concern or issue, including environmental protection, better working conditions, civil rights, discrimination, war, AIDS, homelessness, abortion, or the rights of animals, Native Americans, women, and homosexuals.

Nonviolent methods are also an effective way to deal with local concerns. To protest the danger of a toxic-waste facility situated close to an elementary school and residential neighborhood in East Liverpool, Ohio, residents of the small town mounted a relentless nonviolent campaign of petitions and protest demonstrations.

Conversely, nonviolent action is a powerful tool to apply to broad international issues, such as human rights. Until South Africa ended apartheid, for example, people in many different nations protested the white minority government's policies of racial discrimination and segregation of South African blacks.

Conflict. Conflict and the struggle to resolve it are part of the human condition. Too often, though, individuals, groups, and nations resolve conflict by resorting to violence. Or they reluctantly submit to the other side's demands. Nonviolent action is an alternative both to violence and to submission.

For a variety of reasons, many people ignore a problem or feel powerless to confront it. In 1982, for example, many Americans thought they were powerless to stop the nuclear arms race. To deal with the fear of nuclear war and global pollution, Justine Merritt

asked friends and relatives to design three-foot panels of cloth, on which they would depict, in her words, "what they could not bear to think of as lost forever in nuclear war or global pollution."

As news of the project spread, more and more people grew inspired to participate. Three years later, on August 5, 1985, in commemoration of the atomic bombing of Hiroshima and Nagasaki, Japan,

In memory of loved ones who died of AIDS, thousands of people created sections of this huge quilt, displayed here in Washington, D.C.
RICK REINHARD

thousands of panels were tied together into a seventeen-mile long ribbon, which was wrapped around the Pentagon and other buildings in Washington, D.C. The Ribbon Project has been an ongoing action throughout the world, with Ribbon events occurring in South Africa, Israel, Sri Lanka, Japan, and elsewhere.

By protesting the danger of nuclear war and global pollution in such a gentle, symbolic action, thousands of people who would otherwise not have carried out direct actions empowered themselves and became connected to a larger community of people who shared their concern.

Choice. People can choose between violence and nonviolence. Some people choose nonviolent action for ethical reasons: A method that avoids hurting or killing is morally superior to a method that inflicts violence. In fact, for some people, nonviolent principles guide all aspects of their lives, from the food they choose to eat (or not eat), where they live, and how they earn their livelihoods, to how they direct their taxes, and the issues and causes they champion.

Most people, however, choose nonviolent methods because they lack the means, resources, or confidence in their ability to use violence. For them, nonviolence is simply a practical technique, not a moral compass.

Although labor leader César Chávez was deeply committed to nonviolent principles himself, Chávez took a practical stance toward the impoverished migrant workers whom he organized into the United Farm Workers Union. "We're not nonviolent because we want to save our souls," he explained. "We're nonviolent because we want to get some social justice for the workers. . . . What do the poor care about strange philosophies of nonviolence if it doesn't mean bread to them?"[5]

Even if they have the means, resources, and confidence to use violence, people often choose nonviolent action because it is less costly and more efficient. Or, the use of violence would incur such public outrage that the practical consequences of nonviolent action make it a preferable technique.

When people choose nonviolence for practical reasons, then it is called practical (or tactical) nonviolence. When they choose nonviolent action for moral reasons, it is called principled nonviolence.

In practical nonviolence, nonviolent methods are merely a means to an end. But principled nonviolence, which requires a strong faith in nonviolence, emphasizes the moral side of conflict. Consequently, winning isn't the ultimate goal; creating a loving community and living a life of integrity is.

Most nonviolent actions are driven by practical concerns. Likewise, many political movements combine both nonviolent and violent sanctions together in their strategy. The Intifada movement of the Palestinians, for example, is better known for its rock throwing and acts of terrorism than for its nonviolent sanctions. Yet since the 1930s, and especially since the Palestinian National Council meeting in 1987, some Palestinians have used nonviolent methods, such as labor strikes, boycotts, and tax resistance alongside their armed struggle against Israel.[6] "We're no longer seen as a violent, terrorist people who are bent on armed struggle and destroying Israel," wrote Souad Dajani, a professor at the University of Jordan, of the Palestinian *intifada* movement, "but rather we're perceived more as a people with a legitimate national cause engaged in unequal struggle against an occupation regime."[7]

Similarly, a person may choose nonviolent action for one cause but not for another. For instance, a person may participate in a nonviolent campaign to stop construction of a mall on a wetland yet willingly serve in the military and use violence to stop oppression.

Most people believe that they have a right to use violence and don't know much about nonviolence or trust that it can work for them. If they appreciated the *power* of nonviolent action and understood how to use it to their advantage, perhaps many of these same people would choose nonviolent methods instead.

Some people lack the skills and experience to overcome their fears about doing certain types of actions, such as mass demonstrations. Yet if they realized that broadening their knowledge of nonviolent strategy and tactics could improve their skills, as well as their chances of winning, perhaps they, too, would choose to use nonviolent methods more often.

Still others who know a considerable amount about nonviolent methods occasionally choose violence over nonviolence because they believe that it is more effective or appropriate for a particular situation. During the American abolition movement of the mid-nineteenth century, for example, many abolitionists who were committed to pacifism (refusing to take up arms) supported the Civil War after losing any hope of ending slavery with nonviolence. Or, as one activist from ACT UP, the gay action group committed to the AIDS issue, admitted, "If violence would work, I would use it."

In some conflicts, a few people choose neither violence nor nonviolence, but submission instead. As the ethnic conflict between the Serbs, Croats, and Muslims in Bosnia raged on during the mid-1990s, David McReynolds, a pacifist and member of the War Resisters League, believed that both violence and nonviolence were futile responses to the Bosnian conflict. "It is difficult to realize that not all problems have solutions," McReynolds explained of his rather dismal outlook. "Not all crimes can be stopped."[8]

Power, conflict, choice. Together they define nonviolent action. And nonviolent action is the power of people. Sometimes people use nonviolence instinctively. More often, though, they choose it. Regardless of the reasons—moral or practical—nonviolence has the best chance of success when practiced by those who know what nonviolent action is and how to use it effectively.

CHAPTER

2

Playing by the Rules

Hope has two beautiful daughters. Their names are anger and courage: Anger at the way things are and courage to see that things do not remain the way they are.

—*St. Augustine*

Mention nonviolence to uninformed people and they often picture people who are short on guts and long on idealism. A bunch of long-haired, long-winded peaceniks praying for world harmony, living together on love and tofu, and ardently committed to saving the rain forest and the spotted owl.

The better informed think of Mohandas Gandhi's nonviolent mass movement to free millions of Indian citizens from British rule or Martin Luther King Jr.'s struggle for civil rights.

How wrong or incomplete such images are. So wrong that nonviolent leader Mohandas Gandhi felt the need to coin a new word—*satyagraha* (which means "truth force")—that would more accurately convey the principle of nonviolence. In order to set aside erroneous myths, and to present a comprehensive portrait of people power, as nonviolent action is often called, consider what nonviolence is and what it isn't.

Nonviolent activists do not use violence.

Refusing to physically injure or kill anyone is the most basic nonviolent principle. Some people extend this principle to mean avoiding inflicting *all* harm, including verbal insults, property damage, and even the *threat* of harming anyone or anything.

Most nonviolent activists, however, draw the line at people and their physical well-being. Thus, even if they damage property to stop a greater harm, all nonviolent direct actions require the commitment to refrain from personal assault.

Nonviolent action means refusing to back down in the face of violence.

Nonviolent action is a difficult place for cowards. While many direct actions, such as leafletting or protest marches, are relatively safe, many others are not. Striking workers have suffered the loss of paychecks and jobs. Nonviolent protesters have been attacked by dogs, angry mobs, hostile police, and military force. Some activists get dragged by their hair or limbs, beaten, blackmailed, tortured, maimed, or killed. In highly repressive political climates, activists have suffered such treatment merely for meeting together, penning a letter, making a critical statement, or even for praying. After they were caught distributing pamphlets and painting slogans that warned against the evil occurring in Nazi Germany in 1943, German students Sophie Scholl and her brother, Hans, were arrested and charged with high treason. Within five days of their arrest, the two young dissidents were beheaded.

For distributing pamphlets denouncing Nazism, German university student Sophie Scholl and her brother, Hans, were beheaded in 1943. DR. GEORGE J. WITTENSTEIN, COURTESY OF THE UNITED STATES HOLOCAUST MEMORIAL MUSEUM

Because of the risks, participants in nonviolent action need to develop discipline, restraint, and the ability to overcome fear. Though not always a guarantee, such stoicism and resolve can greatly empower participants of a nonviolent direct action or movement. It can also serve other purposes as well.

First, nonviolence is such a stark contrast to violence that it makes an opponent's violence look unfair, brutal, and even savage. This, in turn, can rouse public opinion against the violent opponent. It can also prompt the opponent who is meting out the violence to question, and perhaps stop, inflicting such harm on people who restrain themselves from inflicting violence.

When opponents have reason to believe that the other side will remain nonviolent, they have less reason to panic and use violence in the first place. For example, if past experience with a particular group assures police that demonstrators are unlikely to use any violence, the police will feel more secure about maintaining order and less inclined to threaten protesters with tear gas or force.

Even a one-sided commitment to nonviolence, while risky, generally incurs fewer injuries and deaths than violent struggles. Minimizing violence also makes it easier to stay in the fight longer or to retreat from a particular battle to regroup and plan new actions.

Finally, refusing to back down in the face of violence is a powerful weapon itself. When opponents realize that no matter how much they bully a nonviolent group, no matter how many people get arrested, beaten, or killed, more and more will take their place, such resolve erodes both the opponents' confidence and power.

Nonviolence can be defined as active, never passive.

Nonviolent action may require passively *resisting* violence, but it hardly ranks as passivity itself. In fact, nonviolent action means what it sounds like: taking *action* to resolve a conflict, confront an issue, and correct a problem. It also means refusing to be indifferent, submissive, or apathetic.

When state officials decided to transport 7,223 truckloads of soil laced with PCB—a toxic, cancer-causing substance—to a landfill in North Carolina, they never expected opposition from residents of

Warren County, which was one of the poorest in the state. To their surprise, however, Warren County citizens organized a massive protest that resulted in the arrest of more than five hundred protesters who had blockaded the trucks with their own bodies. "They didn't expect us to organize," said one of the protesters, "but we're gonna fight. It's one thing to be poor, it is another to be poor and poisoned."[1]

Because of their commitment to take action, many people find themselves on the cutting edge of an issue. Greenpeace, the environmental action group founded on nonviolent principles, started when two couples decided to protest underground nuclear-bomb testing on Amchitka Island, an area off of Alaska that is prone to earthquakes. They enlisted the help of a few other concerned people.

Sailing into the icy ocean in a small, antiquated fishing boat named *Greenpeace* to "bear witness" to the test put a powerful spotlight on the issue. In fact, it was so powerful that, partly because of public outrage over the testing, the United States Department of Defense stopped using Amchitka as a test area and made it a bird

Demonstrators lie in the road to block transport of highly toxic waste to a landfill in Warren County, North Carolina, where they live.

JENNY LABALME

sanctuary instead. Moreover, Greenpeace burgeoned into a powerful citizen-action group, whose membership now includes millions of concerned people from all over the world.

Nonviolent action does not necessarily require leaders. Leaders of movements, though, tend to take an exceedingly active role. Unlike military generals who can position themselves far from the actual scene of a battle, nonviolent fighting requires leaders to put themselves directly on the front line, where they may be exposed to grave risks, including arrest, jail, and death.

Nonviolent action is not solely used for "good" purposes.

Because nonviolent methods do no bodily harm (although they *can* cause property damage), many people view them as a highly ethical means of fighting. In addition, refusing to commit violence or to back down in the face of violence requires a certain moral fiber.

According to Chris Cook, a member of Greenpeace, being a nonviolent activist in such an organization, where activists scale dangerous heights in order to hang protest banners or plug up pipelines that are dumping toxic waste into rivers or oceans requires bravery, belief in the mission, patience, determination, creativity, and faith in the success of the campaign. "And you have to be decent," adds Cook.[2]

Unfortunately, despite the deeply held moral convictions of many nonviolent activists, nonviolent action does *not* require either moral character or a commitment to virtue. As Christopher Kruegler, an expert on nonviolent strategy, observes, "People using nonviolent sanctions are by no means always the 'good guys.' "[3]

During the height of the Cold War in the 1950s, when fear of communism made the United States and the Soviet Union enemies, anyone suspected of having Communist sympathies or simply being too left-wing, was blacklisted from employment, and their services were boycotted. In this way, many excellent writers, actors, and others in film, television, and book publishing saw their professional lives destroyed by nonviolent sanctions. And to inflict severe economic and social hardships on the Jews of Germany during the Nazi era,

On April 1, 1933, in Germany, many Jewish stores were covered with graffiti that marked them as a place for non-Jews to boycott.
RAPHAEL ARONSON, COURTESY OF THE UNITED STATES HOLOCAUST MEMORIAL MUSEUM

Germany imposed strict boycotts on the sale of Jewish goods and services and used other nonviolent sanctions toward evil ends (though later, the Nazis used large-scale violence against Jews).

Nonviolent action enables the oppressed to gain self-respect and power, the unheard to raise strong voices of protest, the unseen to seize control. But to succeed, nonviolent action requires playing by a certain set of rules—mainly to refrain from using violence and to refuse to back down in the face of violence. Unfortunately, those rules do not always require people to stand on high moral ground or resist evil. On the other hand, nonviolent actions tend to attract people of a certain moral fiber—and inspire them to take an active stand to fight for what they believe is right.

3

People
Power

One of the advantages of nonviolence is that anyone can practice it and we do not need thousands.

—*Larry Gara*

I say nonviolent struggle is armed struggle . . . only with this type of struggle, one fights with psychological weapons, social weapons, economic weapons, and political weapons.

—*Gene Sharp*

When people demonstrate, march, or take over buildings, when they form human blockades, picket, and strike, when they keep long fasts and vigils, when they defy unjust laws and regimes, they use their power much the way soldiers use their weapons. Even people with the most limited physical mobility and resources can tap that kind of "people power."

After several years of unsuccessfully trying to convince Denver's Regional Transportation Department (RTD) to outfit buses with lifts that would enable passengers in wheelchairs to use public transportation, Wade Blank, who had participated in the civil rights and antiwar movements, decided to organize a nonviolent battle.

At 10 A.M. on July 5, 1978, nineteen disabled people in wheelchairs daringly encircled two city buses at the busiest intersection in downtown Denver and refused to leave. Some of the people hurled themselves out of their wheelchairs and lay in the street, blocking traffic. Throughout the day and into the night, the group continued their siege, sleeping in shifts and taking turns keeping the blockade.

Nearly all of the disabled people at the action had spent

their entire lives in their parents' home or in an institution. Most lacked a formal education, money, clout, and confidence. Yet the ability to stop traffic at a busy intersection and draw attention to their cause gave them an incredible weapon.

Over the next year and a half, Blank continued to organize disabled people to fight. In September, pairs of people in wheelchairs positioned themselves at each bus stop on the main route, holding signs that read "WE WOULD LIKE TO GET ON THE BUS." The action caught the attention of both passengers and the press.

Members of the group protested at each monthly meeting of the RTD. On one occasion, they brought Monopoly money to the meeting and said, "You take our tax money, but we can't ride the buses tax dollars pay for."

As the group learned new nonviolent methods, their "arsenal" of weapons expanded, and they grew empowered. "While I was in the demonstration," explains Arthur Campbell, "I felt powerful. Being there, in a group with the same people after the same goal was a way to learn the strength that can come from direct action."[1]

After a while, the group established an organization, American Disabled for Accessible Public Transportation (ADAPT), to plan a strategy, recruit more members, gain support, and most of all, to engage in nonviolent action until they achieved their goal.

Each year, ADAPT members carried out a series of protests at the national convention for administrators of public transit systems. As hundreds of transit executives arrived at the convention center, disabled activists wedged their wheelchairs in the doors of the convention hall, blocking the entrance. Others threw themselves out of their wheelchairs, sprawling on the sidewalk to further block access to the building. Still others handed out leaflets explaining their grievances and demands.

When they could enter the main hall, ADAPT members unfurled protest banners and disrupted the speakers by shouting "Access, access, we want access" and similar slogans. On still other occasions, dozens of disabled activists sat in at the offices of government officials and transit administrators, demanding to be heard and heeded and refusing to leave until arrested.

As publicity about their direct actions spread, ADAPT membership grew. In time, they began to gain attention for their issues and concerns and influence legislation. Nevertheless, by March 1990, after years of fighting, their major goal still eluded them. A comprehensive bill that would guarantee access to all public transportation and buildings, and protect against employment, housing, and other discrimination, lay stalled in congressional committee.

To move the bill out of committee and urge its passage, ADAPT members staged a major action. On the first day of the action, more than a thousand people—many of them in wheelchairs—participated in a march along Pennsylvania Avenue, from the White House to the Capitol building. Then, in a symbolic protest, about

To urge passage of the Americans with Disabilities Act, disabled protestors left their wheelchairs and crawled up the steps of the Capitol building.
TOM OLIN/ADAPT

seventy-five disabled activists abandoned their wheelchairs to ascend the eighty-three steep marble steps of the federal building. Eight-year-old Jennifer Keelan, who was born with cerebral palsy, slowly started crawling to the top on her elbows and knees. "I don't care if it takes me all night," Keelan proclaimed.[2]

The next day, others occupied the Rotunda in the Capitol, chaining their wheelchairs together and refusing to leave, an illegal action that forced police to work for four hours, prying apart the protesters with large cutting tools and blowtorches, before they could arrest 104 of them.

Finally, on July 26, 1990, after hundreds of disabled people had carried out heroic protest actions and been arrested; after some of them had been tipped or thrown from their wheelchairs, carried by their necks, or forced into solitary confinement; after much determination, planning, hard work, and many setbacks, the Senate passed the Americans with Disabilities Act (ADA). The ADA guaranteed access to public transportation and public buildings, as well as a host of other civil rights.

With that major victory, ADAPT refocused its efforts on the right to independent assisted living instead of reliance on nursing home care—using its tried-and-true nonviolent arsenal of weapons. Moreover, ADAPT's success inspired disabled activists around the world to use the same methods to fight for similar goals.

ADAPT's story, while unique in many ways, underscores a common theme that runs through most nonviolent campaigns: People band together to use nonviolent methods to gain recognition, strength, support, and above all, to fight some of the biggest, most powerful opponents.

By using nonviolent methods, even one person can successfully battle a giant. Mark Dubois learned that the U.S. Army Corps was planning to fill the New Melones Reservoir, located in California. Fearing that this action would cut off the flow of fresh water to the Stanislaus River and endanger its wildlife, Dubois chained himself to the bank of the river—and risked being drowned—on the day the army intended to fill the reservoir. Because Dubois had publicity for the action and people power behind him, the Army abandoned its plans, letting the Stanislaus River maintain its flow of fresh water.

Admittedly, nonviolent methods don't always work. Some groups give up too soon, while others, failing to learn from their mistakes, stay headed on a losing course. Nevertheless, many people, even those who find themselves up against the most powerful opponents, can use people power to fight and win. And as Mark Dubois showed, they can even wage the battle alone.

Power of the People

There are several hundred nonviolent methods, each one a different kind of "weapon" in the fight. Together, they form an entire arsenal of nonviolent weapons, which work by taking varying degrees of power away from an opponent. When a nonviolent method has a detrimental effect on an opponent, it is called a sanction (nonviolent method and sanction are interchangeable words).

Some nonviolent methods have little or no effect. A demonstration that everyone ignores, for example, is hardly effective and therefore constitutes a weak sanction (unless it serves to better empower the people who participated in it). On the other hand, a general strike throughout an entire industry is an exceedingly strong nonviolent sanction.

Many nonviolent actions include more than one nonviolent sanction. To protest construction of a nuclear power plant, for example, an action may include a demonstration march, where activists carry banners and shout slogans or sing protest songs. Other activists may pass out leaflets to bystanders, while still others carry larger-than-life-size puppets in a funeral procession to dramatize the dangers of nuclear accidents and blockade the entrance to the plant. Some activists may even stay at the site of the demonstration for several weeks, carrying out protest fasts and holding prayer vigils. Each one of these behaviors—the march, banners, slogans, singing, leafletting, mock funeral procession, blockade, fasting, and prayer vigils—is a different nonviolent sanction.

In contrast, an action may have only one nonviolent sanction,

Participants of this
"die-in," staged
on an anniversary
of the bombing of
Hiroshima and
Nagasaki, are
protesting the
manufacture of
nuclear weapons.
ELLEN SHUB

such as a "die-in" to protest a war. In this type of action, a small group of people will go to a pedestrian district, such as a park or mall, and on cue, drop to the ground at once, where they lie still, pretending to be dead.

So many people sprawled together on the sidewalk, motionless, is quite a dramatic sight. This action "works" by causing those who witness it to stop and consider the effects of war on civilians trying to carry on with their daily lives. Though simple to do, the die-in has remarkable psychological power.

Successful nonviolent strategies and movements avoid relying on just one method or action. Instead, they use a variety of methods, some of which are more powerful than others. Yet one action or

method may produce exactly the result needed. If the short-term goal of a group is merely to educate the public about an issue, then a public protest letter, creative poster, or symbol, such as a red ribbon to draw attention to AIDS, will suffice.

In his seminal work on the methods of nonviolent action, Gene Sharp compiled a list of nearly two hundred nonviolent methods, which he divided into three categories:[3]

> protest and persuasion
> noncooperation
> intervention

As people learn more about nonviolent action, they can add to the list. Following is a brief explanation of each category and some of the most commonly used methods in each one. All of the categories rely on people power—economic, political, psychological, and social power—and stick to the rules of nonviolent action—no physical violence against other persons and no backing down in the face of violence—to pursue their goals. What distinguishes one method from another is *how* that power is manifested.

Protest and Persuasion

For many years, William and Ellen Thomas maintained a peaceful vigil in Lafayette Park, across from the White House. Bystanders glanced at their banners and occasionally stopped to discuss peace and justice issues with them, read leaflets and pamphlets they had prepared, or sign their petition calling for total United States disarmament and military conversion, which the two tried to get included in a voter referendum.

Each of their methods, from the banner to the petitions, was a *protest* (of United States militarism) or an attempt to *persuade* people to care about the issue and do something about it. Like the Thomases' vigil, this group of actions is done largely to draw attention to a problem or issue, or to air a grievance. These tactics also serve to make known a group's demands.

A sanction may be as simple as one person holding a banner

Because slogans
and posters
clearly express
the reasons for
demonstrating,
they are an
essential part of
most direct actions.
LAWRENCE FRANK/
WAR RESISTERS'
LEAGUE

or painting a slogan on a wall. Or it may be as dramatic as the one
hundred thousand Soviets who risked their lives to gather outside the
Kremlin in order to protest a coup d'état in 1991. It can be as
straightforward as a poster ("War is not safe for children and other
living things") or bumper sticker ("Make love, not war"), as clever as
the mock funeral of Esther Freeman's income tax check (paid the year
of the Gulf War), which was an oversized check painted onto a coffin
decorated with photos of war victims and carried in a funeral procession to her local Internal Revenue Service office on Tax Day[4], and as
easy as forming the peace symbol with two fingers.

When a protest or persuasion garners publicity, it gives
fledgling groups recognition, legitimacy, and strength. When protests
swell with large numbers of people or spread throughout a country,
such as the antiwar demonstrations of the 1960s and '70s in the
United States and the prodemocracy demonstrations throughout Communist countries during the 1980s, they work by undermining the confidence of opponents in their ability to stay in power.

A dramatic photographic image or clever poster can persuade millions of people to change their minds. When Greenpeace showed photographs of bloodstained ice and piles of carcasses left from clubbing baby seals to death, thousands of people who were otherwise indifferent to the fate of the seals supported Greenpeace actions. Likewise, the clever imagery in an advertisement designed by British photographer David Bailey successfully dissuaded many people from purchasing a fur: The ad showed a woman dragging a fur coat that leaves a trail of blood, with the caption, "It takes up to forty dumb animals to make a fur coat. But only one to wear it."[5]

Hundreds of thousands of people participating in a single action can draw remarkable attention to a group and its cause. ELLEN SHUB

Another significant purpose of these methods is to galvanize support, recruit new members, and boost morale. After the Stonewall Riot of 1969 in New York City, in which homosexuals who had been harassed by police fought back, the gay community organized its first protest march, held in Washington, D.C. This march not only gave homosexuals a public forum for airing their grievances, but it gave many participants confidence in themselves and the support of a community of people willing to fight for their rights. In fact, the march encouraged many gay people who had kept their sexual preference a secret from even close family members and friends to come out of the closet, so to speak—to reveal their true sexual identity—and be proud of themselves.

The list of protest and persuasion methods is as endless as a person's imagination and as familiar as the evening news. When they need more powerful sanctions, however, many groups turn to the second category of nonviolent weapons—noncooperation.

Noncooperation

In this second group of methods, people refuse to cooperate or do what is expected of them. Because they put serious pressure or coercion on opponents, these methods can be extremely powerful.

One of the most common methods of noncooperation is the strike. To support an unpopular school tax, teachers may only need to *threaten* to noncooperate by striking in order to convince taxpayers to vote for the tax. Likewise, to protest a government, voters can stay away from the polls en masse to show their disapproval and lack of support.

Noncooperation tactics may be legal or illegal. Workers who strike a car manufacturer may be within the law, while sailors who strike against the Navy would be guilty of mutiny or sedition. Both groups risk losing their paychecks or jobs, but striking sailors are breaking the law and therefore risk losing their freedom as well.

The other most commonly used noncooperation method is the boycott, in which large numbers of people withhold their participation. In an economic boycott, people who would ordinarily buy a

Noncooperation takes many forms, but some of the most common are boycotts, strikes, and work stoppages. Here, the late labor leader César Chávez urges a boycott of California grapes in order to improve the plight of the grape pickers he represented.
ELLEN SHUB

product or use a service stop doing so. (An embargo is when one nation demands that its citizens boycott the products or services of another nation or group of nations.) An eight-year boycott of General Electric products, especially of their hospital equipment, pressured one of the largest multinational corporations in the world to stop manufacturing neutron bombs and sell off its nuclear-weapons parts division.

Boycotts often require huge sacrifices and force people to make difficult decisions. For years, black athletes from South Africa boycotted major athletic competitions to protest apartheid. And the Olympic Committee boycotted all South African athletes from participating in the summer Olympics. Likewise, South African artists were boycotted from participating in a prestigious international art competition, the Biennale.

Strikes, boycotts, and other methods of noncooperation have been the mainstay of many mass movements, including both the labor and the civil rights movements. They are often used in conjunction with other methods, especially protest sanctions. For the most part, their power comes from numbers: The more people who participate in a strike or boycott, the greater its effect will be on an opponent. As such, they require good organizational skills, the ability to inspire and motivate people to noncooperate, and the determination to sustain a strike or boycott as long as possible.

Intervention

In this last group of methods, activists do what they are *not* supposed to do. For example, no one is expected, or legally permitted, to lie across a road and block traffic. Nor are people expected to stop eating (fasts), take over buildings, destroy property, or overload a system (by planning for large numbers of people to get arrested and refuse bail, for example).

By disrupting meetings and business, destroying property, and forming alternative governments and institutions, activists actually coerce, or force, their opposition to give into their demands. Or they may even force their opponents "out of business" or existence altogether. In fact, because intervention methods rely on such force, they differ from violent sanctions only in their commitment to cause no physical injuries or death to people.

One of the most unique methods in this group is the fast, in which activists refrain from eating any food in order to protest an unjust situation. Another important method is the occupation, in which activists seize a building or illegally occupy a site, refusing to leave until their demands are met. Using this method, civil rights workers successfully desegregated many public facilities in the South during the 1960s, including restaurants, amusement parks, and movie theaters.

Unlike the other two groups of sanctions, methods of intervention sometimes include the destruction of physical property. For example, Greenpeace activists sprayed the coats of baby seals with harmless green paint in order to devalue the fur on the market and save the baby seals from being hunted.

Another method in this group involves replacing institutions or governments. To protest Israeli occupation of what they considered to be Palestinian territory, the *intifada,* a Palestinian resistance group, set up their own schools and parallel institutions to lessen Israeli control over their lives.

Because these methods can be so disruptive and destructive, they risk alienating the very people that a protest group needs to support its cause. But when achieving certain goals is independent of gaining public approval or support, many activists resort to intervention methods without compunction. People from Earth First!, a radical environmental group, drive stakes into trees, which can cause loggers to break their saws. Their goal is not to win public approval, but rather to save trees, and to that extent, it is a powerful sanction.

Because they *are* so disruptive, dangerous, and powerful, these sanctions should never be undertaken lightly or for frivolous causes. At times and under certain conditions, they can rival or even surpass the most violent sanctions in resisting oppressive governments and achieving nearly insurmountable goals. In fact, intervention done by masses of people can dismantle an entire government or create a climate of terror. But used toward good ends, it can accomplish the most heroic feats.

Nonviolent sanctions are to nonviolent activists what bullets and bombs are to soldiers. Loaded with people power, they can be extremely effective. To be sure, the most powerful sanctions should be used with caution and reserved for important issues.

Knowing how to do many nonviolent sanctions and knowing how to do them well increases a group's overall strength. And with that strength, the chance of victory dramatically improves as well.

4

Mark of
Distinction

Who is a hero? The person who controls the urge to hate. Who is a hero among heroes? The person who controls the urge to hate and who makes his or her enemy a friend.

—*Talmud*

God sits in the man opposite me; therefore to injure him is to injure God himself.

—*Mohandas Gandhi*

Although principled nonviolence and tactical nonviolent action both rely on the same methods, principled nonviolence has a unique mark of distinction: respect for the enemy. Some of the most successful nonviolent mass movements, including the civil rights movement, the peace movement, and India's nonviolent mass movement for freedom from Great Britain, have been guided by principled nonviolence. Yet many nonviolent movements are driven by practical concerns, and some are driven by a desire for victory at any cost.

Although leaders such as Martin Luther King Jr. admonished their followers to have respect for their enemies, this principle is most easily applied to personal conflicts and confrontations, where it produces remarkable results.

No matter how mean-spirited, morally empty, or violent the opponent, the mark of distinction is to value your opponent. This means that even if you strongly disagree or disapprove of your opponent's values, beliefs, or behavior, you *affirm the opponent's worth as a human being.* As the editors of *Direct Action* wrote in 1945 in their

Dr. Martin
Luther King Jr.
implored civil
rights activists to
fight against racial
discrimination
with nonviolent
methods and
always to have
respect for one's
opponent.
LIBRARY OF
CONGRESS

response to the earlier outbreak of World War II, "There must always be an uncompromising practice of treating everyone, including the worst of our opponents, with all the respect and decency which they merit as fellow human beings."[1]

Perhaps the easiest way to understand this principle is to consider prisoners' rights. In a democracy such as ours, even those who have committed the most bestial crimes are accorded minimum standards of decency—a fair trial, food, clothing, medicine, and shelter *just because they are human beings,* if for no other reason.

For nonviolent activists, the primary way to show respect is by refusing to physically harm or kill an opponent, or even threaten to do so, regardless of the circumstances. But respect can be shown in other ways too. Many principled activists believe that *their* own willingness to suffer with dignity rather than *cause* any suffering shows respect.

Another essential way to show respect is through good communication and the willingness to see your opponent's perspective. This requires tolerance, open-mindedness, and understanding, even when you strongly disagree or disapprove. Let's say that you are committed to saving the whales. Showing respect requires that instead of denigrating the whalers themselves, you show compassion for their need to earn a livelihood and awareness of their difficulty in finding an alternative occupation to whaling.

Unfortunately, respect is often a one-way street. Despite the restraint that civil rights workers maintained for their oppressors, they were often treated with brutality, hatred, and violence.

Some nonviolent activists even try to love their enemies. After his home was firebombed during the Montgomery bus boycott, Martin Luther King Jr. refused to abandon his principles. "We must love our white brothers no matter what they do to us," he insisted. "We must meet hate with love."[2]

In this protest against construction of a nuclear power plant in New England, a demonstrator is making eye contact with the police, perhaps to encourage them to be more compassionate and understanding.
ELLEN SHUB

This kind of love is called *agape* and means honoring the holiness in everyone by recognizing that each person is a child of God. Or as Dr. King explained, "When we love on the *agape* level, we love men not because we like them, not because their attitudes and ways appeal to us, but because God loves them."[3]

Respect your enemies? *Love* them? Does this make any sense? And given human nature, is it even possible?

How can we respect those who refuse to recognize us or take our grievances seriously? Who would set attack dogs on us, tear-gas us, poke us with cattle prods, or even kill us? Who distort the system of justice with unfair laws and harsh, cruel punishment? Why *love* anyone who violates our rights, hates us, seeks to destroy us, is mean-spirited, misguided, or evil? Isn't such unconditional acceptance a violation of *our* right to self-respect, self-worth, and justice?

Certainly, respect for enemies radically departs from the way most of us have learned to deal with conflict and injustice. Despite familiarity with the Golden Rule—that we treat others as we would have them treat us—our usual response is to fear or hate anyone who hurts or threatens to hurt us, denies us our rights, or tries to defeat or destroy us.

We also learn to depersonalize our opponents, to treat them as the "other." Instead of emphasizing what we have in common, we set ourselves apart from them by focusing on our differences. We learn to call them derogatory names. The Nazis even called their prisoners by number, as if they had no name, no personhood, no membership in the human race.

From personal conflicts to warfare, the whole idea of respect and love for opponents seems absurd. When Palestinian leader Yasser Arafat shook Israeli Prime Minister Yitzhak Rabin's hand in peace in 1993, after so many decades of mutual hatred, distrust, and violence between Israel and the Palestinians, the gesture seemed preposterous and totally against human nature. In fact, most people who claim to love or forgive their worst enemies are usually regarded as too idealistic or saintly. Such behavior, after all, defies what we feel or the logic we have been taught.

Neither respect nor love for an opponent requires that we be blind to their faults or tolerate their mistreatment of us. "I love them," explains David Dellinger, "but that doesn't stop me from being angry. I love everyone, but don't necessarily want to join forces with them. I love them, but I don't *like* them or the things they are doing."[4]

Nor does respect for an enemy require that we absolve people of their moral shortcomings, or stop getting angry at them. Loving people, as pacifist A. J. Muste pointed out, does not "require our cooperation in their lying or exploitation or some other evil thing that they do."[5]

Indeed, we *should* hold people accountable for their actions and we *should* be angry with injustice and cruelty, apathy and antagonism, with racism, prejudice, and terrorism. How we choose to express that anger and resolve those issues is essential though. For we need to learn to control our hatred and channel our anger in constructive ways.

Many people believe that every person has the potential for violence and hatred, that such behavior and feelings are natural. Yet a few societies exist that have little violence or war, or even common words for these concepts.[6] Moreover, even *if* violence and hatred are natural, principled nonviolence requires *going against that nature or behavior and learning how to control it in order to do what is right.* Just as we can control our greed or sexual desire, we can learn to suppress our hatred and direct our anger into constructive, rather than destructive, means.

Furthermore, many principled nonviolent activists believe that it is wrong and unnecessary to humiliate, conquer, or destroy an enemy. They seek to transform the entire conflict and reconcile their differences with peaceful solutions—"win-win" victories instead of the traditional for-every-winner-there-has-to-be-a-loser mentality.

Making a friend out of an enemy is far more productive and ethical. "If I make a friend out of an enemy," Abraham Lincoln once said, "I no longer have the enemy." Short of that achievement, these kind of activists strive to change their opponents' *behavior,* and not to destroy an opponent altogether.

For Goodness' Sake

If we are to confront what is wrong in our lives, conflict is unavoidable and fighting to resolve those conflicts is imperative. On the other hand, we can limit our agenda to major issues and ignore the many petty ones that crop up. And by choosing to fight nonviolently, we elevate conflict resolution to a "higher moral plane." As Martin Luther King Jr. reminded us, nonviolence can keep you from sinking as low as your enemy.[7]

Treating others with respect inspires them to see the good in themselves and can, in the best of circumstances, "awaken a sense of moral shame" in them when they suddenly see how awful *their* violence contrasts to our nonviolence and decency toward them.[8]

During the civil rights struggle, courage to restrain from violence was tested again and again. Here, attack dogs were turned on demonstrators in Birmingham, Alabama.
AP/WIDEWORLD
PHOTOS

Many critics claim that nonviolent tactics cannot succeed in bringing out the moral good in anyone who lacks moral decency in the first place. They believe that people surrender not because they have a moral change of heart, but out of necessity. Employers, for example, rarely give in to striking workers' demands or consumers' boycotts because they have a change of heart. Instead, they bring a conflict to an end by "giving in" because if they don't their financial losses will continue and may even drive them out of business. But principled nonviolent activists maintain that practicing nonviolence against even the worst of enemies is right because it brings out the moral best in *themselves.*

That few people accept these "lofty" principles of respect and tolerance for one's enemy or have the moral strength they require should not dissuade anyone from striving to reach them. After all, to achieve any idealistic goal, the reach must be far greater than the grasp.

On the Practical Side

Of course, not everyone who practices nonviolent action has concern, respect, or love for their enemies. Indeed, some activists can be so self-righteous about their cause that they are unwilling to listen to any other viewpoint. Yet even for them, treating opponents with respect has practical advantages.

First of all, respectful treatment encourages your opponents to acknowledge you and take your grievances seriously. It can also improve conditions *after* a conflict is resolved. Consider how difficult it is to let go of a position if someone attacks you personally, calls you a jerk, tells you that you are stupid, wrong, or bad. In contrast, when someone shows respect for your opinion, even when they disagree with it, aren't you more likely to listen to their side, and even to change your mind if you discover that they have a valid point?

The willingness and ability to see all sides of an issue underscores one of the most important advantages of nonviolent conflict resolution—the use of conflict to expand our own horizons. Just as we believe that our opponents hold wrongful positions or display terrible behavior, we, in turn, might be wrong, if only to a small degree. This willingness to "discover" our own untruths, so to speak, makes principled nonviolence such a mark of distinction.

When Greenpeace workers launched an antifur campaign to stop consumers from buying fur coats, they soon realized that their demands were insensitive to the Inuits (natives of Canada), who depend on hunting wild animals for food and livelihood. In short, by considering a different viewpoint, Greenpeace workers were able to detect some of the shortcomings of their own position.

Respectful treatment of your opponents gives them the confidence that they need not fear or harm you. Whenever activist Ken West is confronted by police or belligerent bystanders at a protest, he tries to strike up a friendly conversation, asking them about themselves, perhaps showing personal snapshots so they can see Ken in a more personal light and realize that he is more like them than not. In this way, West reaches for as personal an interaction as possible. From his many protest experiences, West has discovered that he can often break through the barrier of distrust and ensure his personal safety.

Even the best intention to remain nonviolent and treat opponents with respect can fail, particularly when nonviolent activists confront heartless, brutal antagonists. Still, when respect is present, it elevates conflict to a higher moral plateau and also prevents any violence from escalating further. Given these rewards, it may be a principle worth trying.

5 Breaking the Law to Change the Law

Those who engage in acts of civil disobedience are not saying they do not want laws. They are saying that they want laws to be based on justice for all.

—*Dick Gregory*

Before dawn one day in 1993, Kathy Boylan and three members of her group, the Good News Plowshares, cut through the fence at the Newport News, Virginia, shipyard. Next, they scaled eighty feet of scaffolding to board the U.S.S. *Tucson,* a nuclear submarine under construction.

When they located two of the submarine's Tomahawk missile launchers, they removed the inner metal casings and, using only simple household hammers, proceeded to pound the multimillion dollar launchers, following the biblical dictum to "beat swords into plowshares."

Afterward, the group symbolically poured their own blood onto the launchers, hoping that the shipyard workers would make the connection between blood as a life-sustaining substance and blood shed if the missiles were launched. In this way, the Plowshares activists tried to show shipyard employees that they weren't "just doing a job," but actually building weapons capable of killing millions of people at once.

What motivates ordinarily law-abiding citizens to break the law? What convinces them that their arrest, trials, or prison sentences can solve society's problems?

Following an American tradition as old as the Boston Tea Party, Kathy Boylan broke the law to follow her conscience and help mend society's ills. As she awaited trial, Boylan, who is the mother of five children, explained: "I am haunted by the question 'What would I have done to stop the Holocaust?' Would I have refused to pay taxes to Hitler, or blocked the trains, or hidden the victims, and would I have cut the fence at Auschwitz, crossed the yard, and tried to disarm the gas chamber? I hope so.

"Newport News Shipyard builds death machines, just like German companies built gas chambers. Private property warning should not have stopped German citizens from acting to stop the Holocaust. They can't stop us today."[1]

In the Tradition of Henry David Thoreau

Many direct actions are legal. For numerous reasons, however, activists cannot always achieve their goals by legal means. That is when they resort to "crime" of a very unique nature.

Illegally entering someone else's home is a crime. On the other hand, when a group of people deliberately occupy a building to protest a lack of housing for the homeless, they are breaking the law *in order to take a moral stand.* What sets their action apart from other crime is this moral motivation.

Deliberately breaking a particular law for a moral reason is called civil disobedience, an American tradition that emerged during the nineteenth century after Henry David Thoreau, a teacher, writer, and naturalist, advised people to refuse to pay taxes to a government that, in their view, upheld wrongful policies and immoral laws, such as slavery.

Thoreau believed that neither law nor government has a monopoly on morality. "Is it not possible that an individual may be right and a government wrong?" he asked in 1848, when the United States supported slavery and had militarily invaded Mexico, both

These women are trespassing at a military base in Seneca, New York, in order to take a moral stand against nuclear weapons and militarism.
ELLEN SHUB

actions he believed to be wrong. He assumed no personal duty to make the world a better place, but he refused to commit any wrong, or help anyone else who did, including his government. "If it [government] requires you to be an agent of injustice to another," he advised, "then I say break the law."

Because he opposed the war in Mexico and the laws upholding slavery, Thoreau refused to pay his federal poll tax. No matter how small the tax, he felt that paying it would have made him an accomplice to the government.

The local tax collector gave him this choice: pay a fine or go to jail. Thoreau chose jail. Afterward, he explained his decision in an essay on civil disobedience, in which he advised people to obey their own consciences and disobey immoral laws or policies.

Thousands of people have followed Thoreau's example by refusing to pay taxes that support government policies they believe are wrongful. Others break the law in order to address issues such as civil rights, the arms race, the environment, and the rights of the disabled, animals, women, homosexuals, and the unborn.

An Open Commitment

Although some people practice civil disobedience secretly, most consider it effective and moral only when it is done openly. During the summer of 1981, as war raged in El Salvador, several Salvadoreans from the war zone sought refuge in the Southside Presbyterian Church in Tucson, Arizona, after the United States government had refused to grant them permission to stay, and was planning to deport them back to El Salvador.

When Pastor John Fife learned of their plight, he decided to openly violate United States immigration law. In a letter to the United States attorney general, Fife declared that his church was providing sanctuary for the illegal refugees.

As news of the civil disobedience spread, Sanctuary—the movement to openly harbor refugees—swelled to more than three hundred congregations. Entire cities and one state—Arizona—also joined the movement.

Why did Fife and others break the law so openly? Only by openly challenging the law rather than by secretly harboring the Salvadoran refugees could Sanctuary activists change it. In the long run, changing the law could help far more refugees.

Advantages of Civil Disobedience

Law and order, and the protection of human rights, form the hallmark of a just society and are one of the finest contributions that democracy can make to humanity. When a legal system breaks down citizens go unprotected. Lawlessness, chaos, and disorder prevail. In the 1990s, in Somalia, Africa, millions of citizens suffered starvation, extreme poverty, and violence when local clansmen vied for power and inflicted terror and lawlessness throughout the country.

And with no laws or morality governing personal behavior, Somalian society fell into ruin.

Fortunately, most societies function better than Somalia did in the 1990s. Yet no society has ever reached utopia, or perfection. Until a society does, how can citizens right its wrongs?

The first step in reforming any society is to identify what is wrong in the first place! During biblical times, prophets such as Isaiah and Micah assumed the task of being their society's watchdogs. Our society also has self-appointed watchdogs. Ralph Nader, longtime crusader against industry's wrongs, lectures, writes books, and uses the media to inform citizens about industry's ills and to create public pressure to correct them.

Like the individual watchdogs, organizations such as Greenpeace, which monitors fur trapping, whaling, and transportation of nuclear wastes, may also have the noblest of intentions. Still, does every single person or organization with a conscience or a "moral agenda" have the right to commit civil disobedience? And what if their strong convictions are actually "wrong"? Most complex issues have many sides, after all—and not all sides can be right.

Most ethicists agree that morality is never relative. Goodness and justice come from truth. Nor can popular opinion, majority consent, or power determine that truth. For example, no matter how powerfully the South African government enforced apartheid laws, such laws were never moral because they violated basic human rights.

Furthermore, as complicated issues such as abortion, gay rights, arms control, and environmental protection prove, determining right from wrong can be exceedingly difficult. That difficulty, however, does not excuse us from accepting the challenge.

Martin Luther King Jr. offered a simple test for determining which laws in a society are wrong: "Any law that degrades the human personality."[2] Many activists extend this notion to include any law or policy that threatens life on this planet.

Given all the legal means for alerting us to the problems in our society and to ways of correcting them, why should we resort to civil disobedience?

To thine own self be true. In the truest of Thoreau's spirit, Randy Kehler and Betsy Corner refused to pay their federal income taxes for many years. Kehler explains their tax resistance: "We will not contribute voluntarily to such things as the construction of nuclear bombs and murderous interventions in other countries, which we believe to be criminal and immoral."[3]

To remain true to themselves and their conviction that militarism is wrong, Kehler and Corner pay their state and local taxes, but "redirect" the money they are expected to pay the Internal Revenue Service to causes that they believe the federal government *ought* to support.

To draw publicity to a cause. Legal actions have become so commonplace that they fail to get enough publicity or attention. As a result, many activists resort to civil disobedience in order to attract publicity. A few people, especially if one of them is famous, can garner more press attention with an illegal act than can dozens of legal demonstrators. Likewise, the arrest of thousands often gets international coverage.

To put an issue "on trial." The chance to present their case in court gives activists an effective platform for discussing important

One of the reasons that people resort to civil disobedience is to challenge an unfair law or policy in court.
ELLEN SHUB

issues. In fact, this is actually one of the major reasons for committing civil disobedience.

   People will also carry out civil disobedience in order to bring a case to trial and compel the courts to rule on an issue that the legislature is unwilling or unable to resolve. In this way, civil disobedience hastens social or political change. During the civil rights movement, for example, civil disobedience cases that went to trial forced the courts to strike down laws that treated African-Americans unfairly.

   To give minorities a powerful voice. Some groups choose civil disobedience, especially if large numbers of arrests will occur, because they are too outnumbered to gain power any other way. When AIDS first struck the American gay community in 1982, their minority voice lacked the power or influence to convince legislators to change government policy toward AIDS. Only when members of the gay community founded ACT UP and committed civil disobedience,

Through numerous acts of civil disobedience, gay activists have forced attention to the AIDS crisis and brought about changes in government policies.

ELLEN SHUB

such as illegally occupying medical research labs, did they gain enough power to pressure the government to improve its policy on AIDS.

To put power into the people's hands. Without cooperation and obedience from its citizens, a government is powerless to enforce its laws. If hundreds of thousands of people refuse to obey a law at once, and submit to mass arrests, the judicial system becomes too overloaded to handle all the cases or enforce the law. Then, for all practical purposes, the law is no longer effective.

Civil disobedience can also show people that they have power they didn't realize they had. Many citizens, for instance, believe that only the president and official government representatives can decide which nuclear weapons to dismantle. By using simple hammers to dismantle nuclear weapons and destroy sophisticated satellite surveillance systems, Plowshares activists try to show private citizens that they, too, have the power to disarm.

The Danger of Civil Disobedience

That they break the law openly and willingly accept the legal consequences for their lawbreaking sets civil disobedience apart from ordinary criminals—and, in their opinion, makes what they do right. But is anyone entitled to commit civil disobedience in the first place? And can civil disobedience ever do more harm than good?

As we have learned from the civil rights movement, civil disobedience can improve society. Some people believe that it should be done only when all else fails. Others believe that it should never be used. Indeed, regardless of the best of intentions, how much lawbreaking can or should a society tolerate? Where does civil disobedience end and terrorism and lawlessness begin? What stops disrespect for some laws from leading to disrespect for all laws?

Civil disobedience can be quite destructive. A great deal of destruction has been committed for the sake of virtue, from bombing military recruitment centers and abortion clinics to driving metal stakes through trees to prevent loggers from cutting them down.

Certainly, civil disobedience can inspire a person to act out of principle and courage. But moral certainty also risks self-righteousness or forcing a particular value on others who don't share the same views. Furthermore, done secretly, such as when animal rights activists clandestinely destroy research labs and release caged animals, civil disobedience can create a climate of fear and an atmosphere dangerously close to terrorism.

Civil disobedients risk receiving a punishment that is more severe than they deserve. For disarming a nuclear military silo in 1984, Carl Kabat and Helen Woodson received the longest sentences for nonviolent civil resistance ever given in the United States. Does languishing in jail for years serve a cause as well as being free to solve it through education and legal channels?

If too many groups resort to civil disobedience, or use it for frivolous issues, respect for law and order erodes too far. What if *every* group impatient with the legal process broke the laws they didn't respect or used civil disobedience for less admirable causes?

Finally, when judges rule on a civil disobedience case too narrowly, or only allow the strict facts of the case to be heard and deny defendants the chance to raise broader issues, then civil disobedience backfires and defeats its original purpose.

For example, Randall Terry and several hundred followers of Operation Rescue, an anti-abortion group, blocked entrances to the Atlanta Surgicenter, an abortion clinic in Atlanta, Georgia. Terry and 138 others were arrested. When he refused to pay the thousand-dollar fine, his case went to trial, where he hoped to present the issue of abortion to the court. "You have turned your back on these children," Terry said to the judge, who sentenced him to a year in jail.[4]

"Abortion is not the issue in this case; the issue is trespass and unlawful assembly," the judge replied, shutting off any dialogue that Randall had hoped to have with the court.

Finally, if an act of civil disobedience appears too radical or threatening, it can turn away the very people whom the activist is trying to reach. In 1992, in an individual act of conscience, Lynne Guenther parked her van at the United Nations in New York and demanded that the U.N. create an international sanctuary for war-tax resisters and activists who are persecuted for protesting their governments. Then, to receive media coverage for her idea, she prevented her arrest by holding a can of flammable fuel and a lighter in her hand (which she never intended to use).

"Why would a nice girl like me lock herself inside a van with fuel and lighters in hand?" Guenther asked. "I am not crazier than anyone else, but *I am* fed up. . . . If it is wrong to kill then it must also be wrong to *pay* for killing. International law promises me freedom of conscience."[5] Yet the symbolism of her act backfired when the press portrayed her as a self-destructive, dangerous person.

Civil disobedience is not an easy road to travel nor, as critics point out, always a justifiable one. Activists may spend years in jail, deprived of a normal life and of the freedom to protest legally. For all these reasons, from the price they pay to the risk of eroding respect for the law, many activists resort to civil disobedience only when all other means have failed and only for the most serious issues. But use it they will.

6

For
Appearance's
Sake

*How can they call themselves nonviolent peacemakers,
it is asked, when they are unpeacefully doing violence to
someone else's property?*

—*Colman McCarthy*

Dobbs Ferry, New York, represents the quiet life of small-town America. Its youngsters play in the park, ball fields, and swimming pool in town, all of which are located across the road from the town's medical pavilion, where there is an abortion clinic. In 1990, the town's tranquility ended when Operation Goliath, an intensive anti-abortion crusade, began.

Hundreds of protesters from as far away as California descended on Dobbs Ferry for a series of actions and confrontations, which included constant picketing and blockades in front of the clinic that snarled traffic. As motorists paused at the traffic light, demonstrators thrust pictures of bloody fetuses on their windshields.

In one action, postcards depicting the results of abortion—the remains of the fetus—were mailed to hundreds of households. Other postcards were illegally distributed in Dobbs Ferry's school, in the hope that the schoolchildren would pressure their parents to close the abortion clinic.

At rallies and vigils, anti-abortion protesters carried placards saying "Auschwitz on the Hudson" and delivered soapbox sermons about murdering babies.

In still other actions, protesters chained themselves to the clinic. When they were arrested, they refused to give their names, choosing to spend months in jail waiting for court dates. This cost the taxpayers of Dobbs Ferry a considerable sum of money since extra police had to be hired for the demonstrations, and the town had to pay for excessively long jail time as well as court expenses. Over six years, in fact, Dobbs Ferry estimated that Operation Goliath cost more than one hundred and fifty thousand dollars.[1]

Elsewhere, anti-abortion activists followed suit. When Bill Clinton was on the presidential campaign trail in 1992, Harley D. Belew shoved a plastic box that contained a nineteen-week-old fetus into Clinton's path. "It seems to me that they have shown a great deal of irreverence for a purported human life," lamented activist Father Daniel Berrigan. "Their whole point is just to appall good people, and that speaks for itself." But Randall Terry, founder of Operation Rescue, defended the action. "We decided to make Bill Clinton come face-to-face with a victim of choice."

In the last twenty-five years, since the U.S. Supreme Court ruled on *Roe* v. *Wade,* the decision legalizing abortion, more than a thousand acts of violence against abortion providers have occurred. Nearly one hundred clinics have been bombed or burned to the ground. When Dr. Harold Kelly, an abortion provider, left his home to go to work, nearly eighty protesters greeted the physician with songs, prayers, and signs that read "DR. KELLY KILLS CHILDREN."

No matter how offensive such campaigns are, they work. By 1995, more than 80 percent of the counties in America had no abortion providers.[2] According to many doctors, targeting their profession, no matter how crude, is brilliant. "Without the doctor, it [abortion] couldn't happen," said one physician from Cleveland who performs abortions and worries about her safety and that of her family, especially after she was videotaped emerging from the clinic where she performs abortions. "It's a brilliant strategy," she added. "It's very, very effective."

People have the right to exercise free speech, and according to many nonviolent activists, they also have a moral obligation to break the law, if necessary. But how much right do Operation Rescue and similar groups have to continue imposing their views? Does their style of protest offend the very people they seek to convert? Indeed, tactics such as throwing dead fetuses in people's faces can hardly be considered nonviolent.

Over the years, antiwar activists have destroyed nearly a million draft records. Plowshares activists routinely cause hundreds and occasionally millions of dollars worth of damage to federal buildings, weapons plants, missile heads, and communications systems. Animal activists have trashed research labs and freed experimental animals, destroying years of valuable scholarly work.

Is nonviolence truly nonviolent? Is it always appropriate?

Straddling the Fence

Like other proponents of nonviolence, Protestant minister and theologian Reinhold Niebuhr started out being idealistic about the effectiveness and virtue of nonviolent action. But then, after he witnessed the coercion that workers had used during the 1920s labor strikes in Detroit, Michigan, Niebuhr grew less starry-eyed about non-

Despite their stand on high moral ground, demonstrators such as these Plowshares activists, who have defaced a missile with blood, risk alienating would-be supporters.
RICK REINHARD

violent action. Just as violence causes property damage and personal injury, Niebuhr came to understand that methods such as the strike, boycott, and blockade can also be destructive.

But the coercion practiced in nonviolence still differs significantly from violent methods. According to Niebuhr, the difference is a matter of degree. Mark Juergensmeyer, author of *Fighting Fair,* explains it a different way. In his opinion, there are two kinds of coercion—detentive and destructive. Detentive coercion, the kind used in nonviolent methods, is the force used to *prevent* an opponent from doing more harm. During a Greenpeace action, for example, detentive coercion (nonviolent force) would involve destroying the traps that hunters use for catching baby seals. It might also involve spraying the seals' coats with harmless paint in order to destroy the furs' market value and save the seals from being killed.

In contrast, destructive coercion (violent force) would mean blowing up the ships on which the furriers transport the fur; this action would stop the trapping but also kill a number of trappers themselves.

Not only is destructive force inhumane and often "overkill"—for the same goals may be achieved without it—but it destroys any chance of peaceful negotiation and does not help to convince opponents to see your viewpoint. It may even turn off people who have been sympathetic to a cause.

If both detentive and destructive coercion can cause damage or injury, why split hairs over the difference? Because, as Reinhold Niebuhr explained, the *character* of that destruction is essential. Violent force, which is aggressive, causes far more destruction. Furthermore, history has shown that violence tends to lead to more violence. But nonviolent activists, for the most part, remain nonviolent.

There is also an important moral distinction. By not seeking to totally destroy enemies, but rather to appeal to their senses of reason and goodwill, nonviolence is a more ethical way to use force. In contrast, because it attempts to win at the expense of an enemy's loss, destructive force can never be as just or moral as detentive force. And because detentive force is used to minimize damage and to increase the chance of a reconciliation, it can claim far more justice.

As Niebuhr pointed out, nonviolent methods are far from perfect. Still, for most circumstances, they offer the best alternative to violence. Even so, activists need to exercise caution, knowing that even with the best intentions their coercion can be counterproductive, particularly when it too closely resembles the destructive force of violence.

7

When Might Makes Right

If nonviolence does not appeal to your heart, you should discard it.

—*Gandhi*

The international community cannot let 500,000 people be wiped out while peace groups sit around and discuss it.
—*Anne McCarthy*

It is summer 1957, in the small, segregated town of Monroe, South Carolina. You awaken to hot, sticky, muggy days where the sweat beads on your forehead and upper lips and soaks through your clothes. A piercing sun scorches the grass.

Monroe has a municipal swimming pool, built with public money and intended supposedly for public use, a pool that can cool you on the hottest dog day of summer, but only whites are allowed to use it and you are not white.

Robert Williams wants to swim in that pool. He also wants his children and neighbors and friends to swim in it—or in any public pool. Along with other leaders of the African-American community, Williams meets with Monroe town officials to discuss the situation.[1]

"Can we swim in the pool?" Williams asks.

"No," comes the official decision.

"Then can we have a pool of our own?"

"Maybe."

"When?"

"Someday," the officials answer, refusing to commit to exactly when.

"Fifteen years from now?"

"Maybe."

"Can we use your pool a few days a week?"

"No," they tell him. "It'd be too expensive to drain and refill the pool every time your people have used it."

Given this ugly reasoning, Williams and his group decide to picket the pool until they gain permission to use it or the town officials allocate money to build them a pool of their own.

After two days of picketing in the heat, they go on a picnic, deliberately choosing an area that is reserved for whites. Soon, however, a group of white men, already angry about the possibility of desegregating the pool, arrive to harass Williams and his group, firing bullets into the distance to scare them.

Police arrive. Despite the loudness of bullets ricocheting off the trees, the police chief refuses to acknowledge the harassment or do anything to stop it. "Oh, I don't hear anything," he insists. "I don't hear anything at all."[2]

Nor would he take any action against Bynum Griffan, a car dealer who tries to force Williams' car off the road and over a seventy-foot embankment.

After getting no protection from local law-enforcement officials, Williams seeks help from the FBI. They, too, refuse to come to his aid.

For years Williams believed in nonviolence and saw it work. From his experience of living with a lopsided system of justice and Ku Klux Klansmen who spread terror among his people, Williams grew cynical about the effectiveness of nonviolence. Eventually, he decided that in Monroe nonviolence had failed and if he continued to practice it, he would be killed. Seeing no other alternative, he legally armed himself with two pistols and a rifle. Others in his group followed suit.

While nonviolent civil rights workers in other cities were being humiliated, beaten, and even killed, Williams and his group avoided such a fate. Armed with guns, they successfully integrated Monroe's restaurant in only one day—and no one harmed them. "I advocate nonviolence where the law safeguards a citizen's right to peaceful demonstrations," Williams wrote in his memoir, *Negroes with Guns*, "but where there is a break of the law, the individual citizen has a right to protect his person, his family, his home, and his property. To me, this is so simple and proper that it is self-evident."[3]

After carefully observing the civil rights movement and its commitment to nonviolence, Malcolm X, a leader of African-Americans who fought for racial pride and black nationalism, reached the same conclusion. "As a tactic, we approve of nonviolent resistance," he proclaimed. Nonetheless, he failed to see how human dignity could coexist with abuse. "A man cannot have human dignity if he allows himself to be abused, to be kicked and beaten to the ground," he said, "to allow his wife and children to be attacked, refusing to defend them and himself on the basis that he's so pious, so self-righteous, that it would demean his personality if he fought back."[4]

While nonviolent sanctions can produce victories within weeks or even days, many nonviolent campaigns take years, and even decades, to succeed. And certainly, where nonviolence is effective, it is a better alternative to violence. Yet how long is long enough? How much risk or sacrifice should a cause require? And where people suffer extreme injury and loss, or have little chance of success, can nonviolence even be justified?

When Enough Is Enough

Many activists prefer nonviolent resistance and direct action to violent methods, but only as long as they have a remote chance of success. Otherwise, when failure is certain, they believe that nonviolent resistance loses its moral edge and makes tragic martyrs out of people who persist in using it.

Shortly after the Revolutionary War, Quakers and other pacifists turned their attention to abolishing slavery. At first, they appealed to the moral conscience of both slave owners and legislators. Unfortunately, though, no amount of moral reasoning could rock the monolith of American slavery. In fact, the slaves' plight worsened with enactment of the Fugitive Slave Act in 1850, which gave slave owners the right to reclaim a runaway slave, even in free states and territories.

William Lloyd Garrison, founder of the New England Non-Resistance Society in 1839, grew so dispirited about the lack of morality among slaveholders that he urged the use of violence.[5] Even the most stalwart pacifists joined him. As terrible as violence was to them, it was a lesser evil than slavery.

In contrast to these pragmatists, Gandhi never measured the worth of nonviolence by its chance of succeeding. Instead, he believed that nonviolence "is infinitely superior to violence," and sought to "cultivate the quiet courage of dying without killing." In fact, to those who lacked either courage or the means to fight nonviolently, he advised "killing rather than shamefully fleeing from danger."[6] He believed, however, that the results of their struggle can never equal or surpass a victory won through nonviolence.

Not all principled nonviolent advocates take Gandhi's perspective. To them, neither the courage nor the chance of success are the issue. Instead, they believe that the "immorality" of killing or

As this 1817 newspaper ad for a runaway slave illustrates, slavery was so morally reprehensible as to cause a number of pacifists to use violence against slave owners and supporters of slavery. FROM THE COLLECTION OF SIDNEY A. NEIBURG.

800 DOLLARS REWARD.

I WILL give TWO HUNDRED DOLLARS for securing my mulatto servant BEN in any goal, so that I get him again, or the above reward if brought home ; and 2 dollars for the HORSE he took away with him, the 24 of December last. Ben is a bright mulatto, 17 years of age, of the usual stature of the age, slenderly made, round full face ; thick lips, has a smart beard chiefly on the upper lip, and heavy stupid countenance. Had on when he went away a half worn small brim beaver hat, roundabout and pantaloons of blue cloth, with white metal buttons, and great coat of drab flushing, collar and cuffs faced with dark fur, pieced in the fore skirt.

It is believed to be his intention to get to Philadelphia, where he has a grandmother called Suke, 66 years of age, about 5 feet high, and an aunt called Rachel 36 years of age 5 feet 6 or 7 inches high, both mulattoes, born slaves in the state of Maryland, lived a few years in Alexandria, state of Virginia, were manumitted and removed to Philadelphia some 8 or 10 years back. The horse is a dark bay, 10 or 12 years old, about 13 hands high, cropped tail and ridged mane. Masters of vessels and others were forewarned from employing or carrying off said servant, at their peril.

DENNIS MAGRUDER,
Ten miles east of Washington City.

April 14

intentionally injuring any living thing prohibits them from condoning violence, no matter the circumstances.

In the 1970s, members of the nonviolent community in Nicaragua abandoned their commitment to nonviolence and joined the armed resistance to President Anastasio Somoza. Even though they had killed several guards, Ernesto Cardenal, cofounder of the community, defended their action. In fact, he referred to them as "those young Christians who fought without hate—and especially without hate for the guards" they had killed.[7] Father Daniel Berrigan, a staunch opponent of militarism and the use of violence, sharply criticized Cardenal's reaction. In Berrigan's opinion, no matter how righteous a person's intentions are, killing never has any merit or virtue. "Alas," he lamented in a letter to Cardenal, "I have never seen anyone morally improved by killing; neither the one who aimed the bullet, nor the one who received it in his or her flesh."[8]

According to Berrigan, we have the choice to take up arms or refuse them, suffering the consequences of either decision. "One says no [to killing] when every ache of the heart would say yes," Berrigan concedes. "But if we take up arms, regardless of how noble the cause, we simply disappear in the bloody, secular history of the world."[9]

Nonviolent struggles often require Herculean efforts and a great deal of patience. Nonviolence works if it is given enough commitment and effort, enough time and "experimentation with every possible alternative," according to longtime activist and folksinger Joan Baez. And if it should fail, reasons Baez, "The only thing that is a worse flop than pursuing nonviolence is the organization of violence."[10]

Pacifists like Berrigan and Baez refuse to straddle the fence and have it both ways: Either people hold fast to their nonviolence or take up arms and wear blood on their souls.

For many people, however, virtue is rarely so clear-cut. There are numerous considerations—not only the chance that nonviolence can succeed, as well as its risks and sacrifices, but also the moral nature of your foe. If your enemy is indecent, then, in their opinion, to rely on nonviolent action is tantamount to suicide.

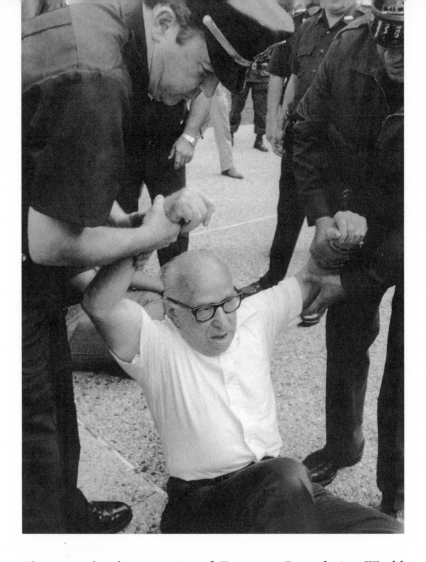

Regardless of the
circumstances,
those deeply
committed to
nonviolent
principles believe
that nonviolence
is superior to
violence.
ELLEN SHUB

Observing the dire situation of European Jews during World
War II, German-Jewish philosopher Martin Buber was unwilling to
bet Jewish fate on nonviolence. When Gandhi exhorted the Jews
to remain nonviolent against Hitler, Buber countered that nonviolent
resistance in such circumstances is wrong. Writing prophetically to
Gandhi in 1939, several years before the fate of Europe's Jews was
sealed by Hitler's "Final Solution," Buber asked: Is it better to die
virtuous or to live?

Faulting Gandhi for trying to draw a parallel between British
and Nazi oppression, Buber told Gandhi that bringing opponents who
have moral fiber "to their senses" is a realistic challenge. In contrast,

expecting to appeal to the moral conscience of a "diabolical universal steam-roller [such as Hitler] is tantamount to mass suicide." Besides, asked Buber, what moral compass could demand such a sacrifice?[11] Judaism, Buber explained, believes that people have the right to use force when there is no alternative way to defend themselves or their families. "We should be able even to fight for justice, but to fight lovingly."[12]

Having It Both Ways

Instead of pursuing nonviolence for moral reasons, most people use nonviolent methods because they have no other recourse or because nonviolence offers them a winning edge. In fact, some scholars estimate that the majority of nonviolent action is done out of pragmatism, not idealism.[13] However, a lack of strong moral commitment to nonviolent principles increases the risk that participants will eventually resort to violence.

In their long struggle for equal rights, South African blacks teeter-tottered between nonviolence and violence. Though the South African government had never been known for racial tolerance, in 1911 it passed the first of many laws that stripped black citizens of their civil rights, including the right to own land or participate in government.

A year later, in response to their bleak situation, black activists founded the South African Native National Congress, later known as the African National Congress (ANC), the first national liberation movement created on the African continent. For the next fifty years, the ANC sought to achieve full equality exclusively through nonviolence.

After unarmed demonstrators were shot at Sharpeville in 1960 and after the government banned all organizations that were fighting apartheid, the ANC ended its absolute commitment to nonviolence. Indeed, faced with an extremely oppressive situation, some activists resorted to guerrilla warfare (the use of surprise tactics by small groups in enemy territory).

When the government responded to this new militancy with

a long wave of terror and oppression, anti-apartheid groups only strengthened their conviction that liberation required an armed struggle. As a result, during the next three decades, they sharply escalated their use of violence.

Meanwhile, in the late 1970s, a powerful black trade union movement emerged—the Confederation of South African Trade Unions, which used nonviolent methods. When the Confederation joined with other anti-apartheid organizations to form a broad coalition, called the United Democratic Front, nonviolence gained more power. Using strikes, boycotts, and other nonviolent sanctions, which climaxed in the Defiance Campaign of 1989, the United Democratic Front compelled the government to reform and eventually abolish its racist policies. Thus, although the struggle to erase apartheid included violence, nonviolence played an important role.

In the thirteenth century, St. Augustine outlined the first modern moral justification for war. For a war to be just, he claimed, it had to be declared by a legitimate authority, such as a government. Moreover, it had to be fought for a just cause, with the right intentions, in a proper manner, and only as a last resort. Finally, only wars of defense, not wars of aggression, could be morally justified.[14] Now that our modern weapons of war have the capacity to extinguish all human life, many people can no longer find any justification for war.

Others trust the military *not* to slide down the slippery slope to nuclear annihilation, and instead suggest that war can be limited. Even so, they believe that violence should be used only for the most compelling moral reasons. According to political scientist Michael Walzer, author of *Just and Unjust Wars,* violence is justified if it is used to put an end to horrific situations that "shock the moral conscience of mankind."[15] In fact, Walzer argues, we not only have the right to use violence for humanitarian reasons, but if we have the means to stop such monstrosities, the duty as well.

For some people, nonviolence is all-or-nothing—stick to non-violent sanctions, no matter what the situation or how steeply the cards are stacked against you. And if you can't go "all the way" with nonviolence, take up arms and fight like a trooper.

Most people, however, reject such rigid standards and straddle the fence instead. When nonviolent action is a justifiable moral alternative, they use it. In the face of certain defeat or grossly inhumane situations, they don't. And for some people, of course, the issue isn't moral at all—they choose whatever course of action is most likely to succeed.

2

Learning
To Do
Nonviolent
Action

8 Learning the Way of the Warrior

Nobody was born nonviolent. None was born charitable. None of us comes to these things by nature, but only by conversion. The first duty of the nonviolent community is helping its members work upon themselves and come to this conversion.

—*Lanza del Vasto*

To feel anger and fear while participating in a nonviolent action is natural. In order to succeed, though, nonviolent activists need to restrain themselves from using violence, even when violence is used against them. Those who organize actions and campaigns also must know as much as possible about nonviolent action so they can choose the methods that will work best, get needed publicity and support, and map out an entire nonviolent campaign. This, of course, is a tall order.

Just as military troops are trained to fight, nonviolent activists are trained to fight nonviolently. For some, training is direct. ADAPT, the disabilities activist organization, for example, believes in training people by engaging them in a real direct action, such as carrying out a sit-in at a restaurant that has no ramps for wheelchairs. Most nonviolent activists, however, feel that advance preparation, through lectures, workshops, and simulated actions, improves the odds of success, as well as reduces the chance of violence.

On December 1, 1955, in Montgomery, Alabama, Rosa Parks, an African-American woman who was returning home from a hard day's work as a seamstress, was too weary to give up her seat to a white person, even after the driver asked that she stand and move to the back of the bus. Mrs. Parks still refused to budge, so the driver reported her to the police, who arrested her. After spending a night in jail, Mrs. Parks was released on bond.

As soon as several women learned of her arrest, they phoned E.D. Nixon, a leading civil rights activist, and proposed that he initiate a boycott of the bus system to correct the injustice black passengers had to face.

Nixon called a young minister, Dr. Martin Luther King Jr., and asked him to organize a bus boycott, which lasted more than a year and started a powerful protest movement. Rosa Parks innocently claimed that she didn't really know why she refused to give up her seat that day, and Dr. King had only responded to a request. Yet both of these pivotal figures in the civil rights movement had been well prepared for what did occur.

Mrs. Parks was a seasoned civil rights worker. In fact, just a month prior to her refusal to give up her seat, she had attended a leadership seminar at the Highlander Folk School in Tennessee, which was the principal training center in the South for union organizers. At the seminar, she learned how to use strikes, boycotts, and other nonviolent tactics to improve working conditions and wages. Furthermore, when Mrs. Parks decided to remain in her seat on the bus, she was clearly aware that her action was a "sit-in" and that she needed to remain calm, dignified, and brave because she was surely going to be arrested.

Dr. King, too, had attended Highlander, and had read widely about nonviolent theory and practice long before he led the bus boycott. Because they were prepared for nonviolent action, both Mrs. Parks and Dr. King made immeasurable contributions to the cause of justice.

The Value of Training

Remaining calm during a nonviolent action, refusing to retaliate when someone hurts you, and even learning to endure imprisonment are skills that can be learned. In fact, the success of most nonviolent tactics largely depends on how well participants are trained to remain nonviolent and disciplined, no matter how much suffering they must endure. Training also helps people learn how to plan entire campaigns, an especially important skill if their fight is going to take a long time or is against a formidable enemy. Still another advantage to training is that it brings activists together and helps them form powerful networks.

To learn nonviolent theory, skills, and methods, many people attend training sessions or workshops. Shorter sessions are used for one specific action—a particular demonstration or strike, for example—while longer sessions that last for weeks or months teach people how to organize entire nonviolent campaigns.

Most training sessions start with a history and philosophy of nonviolence, including dispelling myths that nonviolence is passive or cowardly. Participants might also learn more about the particular issue they are supporting, such as nuclear disarmament, AIDS research, disability rights, or threats to the environment.

Most important, however, training sessions teach participants how to put the theory of nonviolence into practice. Through role-playing, sociodrama (acting out a conflict), and other techniques, nonviolent trainees learn the skills necessary to carry out nonviolent direct actions. They also learn what to expect, how to remain nonviolent,

Previous training in nonviolent practice allows these participants to remain calm in the face of their imminent arrest.
ELLEN SHUB

and how to deal with the stress and fear of harassment, physical harm, arrest, and imprisonment. Workshops may also teach participants nonviolent self-defense, decision making, communication skills, public speaking, and conflict mediation, as well as organizing, recruiting, and publicity.

One exercise, for example, is the "hassle line," in which participants form two lines facing each other.[1] As in a debate, one line takes the opposition's side. Then they switch roles. To prepare for a direct action at a nuclear waste disposal site, one line might practice arguing why they have the right to refuse to have nuclear waste buried in their community, while the other side argues the government's position. Then they switch. Hassle lines teach participants to understand their opponent's perspective and to discuss it with them. It also gives them experience in responding to mean-spirited accusations and wrongful assumptions.

As Grace Hedemann, a nonviolent trainer and author of the *Nonviolence Training Manual,* used by the War Resisters League, explains, "Training sets the tone and style of a demonstration, campaign, and movement. It develops confidence, solidarity, and cooperation."[2]

The Making of a Warrior

The custom of training people in nonviolence began during this century's mass movements. In his nonviolent campaign to end British rule over India, Mohandas Gandhi insisted that his followers prepare for direct actions by prayer and fasting, learning to live simply and cleanly, and accepting the nonviolent principles of satyagraha.

In the United States, Richard Gregg proposed the value of training in his book, *The Power of Nonviolence,* first published in 1935, in which he explained Gandhi's theories of nonviolence. Both the labor and the civil rights movements trained volunteers in methods of nonviolent direct action, including strikes and sit-ins.

One of the most influential training programs arose from the Fellowship of Reconciliation, an interreligious group dedicated to settling conflict through nonviolent methods. The Fellowship formed a social action committee to integrate areas surrounding Washington,

D.C., and other major cities and trained volunteers to accomplish that goal.

Within a short while, the social action committee established its own group, the Congress of Racial Equality (CORE), which, in turn, spawned many important nonviolent direct actions throughout the nation, particularly in the South. Through CORE's training, hundreds of volunteers learned nonviolent theory and prepared themselves for sit-ins, Freedom Rides, and other direct actions that occurred during the civil rights campaign.

Trained volunteers successfully integrated the Palisades Amusement Park in New Jersey, a swimming pool and amusement park in Cleveland, and a public bath in Los Angeles.[3] However, they met their most demanding tests when they attempted to use direct action to integrate the South. In fact, the 1961 Ride of Reconciliation to integrate interstate buses and transportation facilities throughout the South was so dangerous that *only* trained and experienced nonviolent activists were permitted to participate, a decision that proved to be wise.

Even when an angry mob of whites attacked the Freedom Riders, they maintained their dignity and refused to retaliate. In fact, despite receiving serious wounds—Jim Peck suffered deep slashes to his head, which required fifty-four stitches, and Dr. Walter Bergman was beaten so badly that he suffered a stroke that left him paralyzed—not a single CORE volunteer ever lost his or her dignity or restraint on that ride.

Sometimes large numbers of people needed to be trained in just a few hours. During the Montgomery bus boycott, for example, thousands of boycotters had to be trained overnight. To meet this challenge, leaders of the boycott, including Martin Luther King Jr. and Reverend Ralph Abernathy, called for meetings at their churches, where they inspired the people with powerful sermons, hymns, and prayers, strengthening everyone's resolve to make the necessary sacrifices and suffer the abuses they would surely encounter. Finally, all participants in the boycott were asked to sign pledges to remain nonviolent throughout its duration.

Even this brief preparation produced remarkable results. No matter how much they were harassed or provoked, the boycotters retained their commitment to nonviolence and to the boycott. As a result, they earned deep respect and a great deal of support for their cause.

Mounting protest against the Vietnam War ushered in a new era of mass demonstrations, too large to train all participants. In May 1970, for instance, hundreds of thousands of people were expected to gather for an antiwar demonstration in Washington, D.C. In response to the huge crowds expected and also to the growing hostility of the police and bystanders, training took a new twist.

This time, a small group of people, called "marshals," were trained to organize the demonstration and maintain nonviolence, mostly by learning to spot troublemakers in the crowd, calm tempers, and deal with hostility before it could escalate. (Today, many demonstrations still use marshals, but they are now called "peacemakers.")

During that same period, several experienced nonviolent trainers published training manuals, such as Jerry Coffin's *Mayday Tactical Manual,* Carl Zietlow and Brian Jaffee's *Training Manual for Nonviolent Direct Action for Spring Actions,* and New Society Press's *Manual for a Living Revolution,* some of which are still in use.

Nonviolent training took still another turn in 1976, when organizers of the Seabrook action in New England to protest the construction of a nuclear power plant once again made training a requirement, even though they were expecting more than a thousand participants. What was unique about their decision was that rather than train a large group at once, they decided to train small groups of ten to twenty persons. Each group would stay together at the action. These small groups, or affinity groups as they are known, have become the cornerstone of many movements today.

First of all, a small group of people who know one another well are in a better position to detect any provocateurs who try to join them. (A provocateur is someone planted by the opposition who tries to incite the group to do something incriminating and therefore sabotage its chance of succeeding. During the Vietnam war protests, for example, the CIA and other government agencies commonly planted provocateurs in student protest groups.)

Being small also allows for a type of decision making called "consensus." Using consensus, a group makes decisions by hearing from each person in the group and arriving at a solution agreed upon by everyone, not just by a majority. An issue is discussed until an agreement is reached. Consensus works best with small groups whose members share common interests and commitments.

Affinity groups make it easier for central planners because each group is responsible for its members' arrests and welfare. In fact, at many demonstrations today, each group may plan its agenda independently of the other groups. One group may pass out leaflets, while several others form a blockade, and still others do a street theater program.

Finally, because members are so familiar with one another and do many direct actions together, it is easier for affinity groups to plan an action. To protest the Persian Gulf War in 1991, for example, an affinity group from Putney, Vermont, met on short notice at a busy shopping street in nearby Brattleboro, Vermont. At a signal, they all

Today, small groups known as affinity groups routinely train and plan for direct actions. Together, affinity groups provide a powerful network of activism.
JOANNE SHEEHAN/ WAR RESISTERS' LEAGUE

lay down on the sidewalk at once, "feigning death." While the protest did nothing to affect any government policy, passersby were forced to confront the issue of war and how its casualties affect ordinary people like themselves.

Plotting a Course

Based on their analysis of nonviolent movements, Peter Ackerman and Christopher Kruegler, authors of *Strategic Nonviolent Conflict,* conclude that many, if not most, activist groups and mass movements would benefit from developing a clear, logical strategy to guide their campaign and direct their movement (an idea familiar to military experts, who have always known the value of a good strategy).[4]

According to Ackerman and Kruegler, a group needs to fill its arsenal with as many nonviolent sanctions as possible. Success also requires the leadership of individuals or committees who can boost morale and make good decisions.

Development of an effective strategy enhances a nonviolent movement's ability to succeed.
RICK REINHARD

As any successful general knows, to succeed, a group needs to study the strengths and weaknesses of both itself and its enemies. The group has to constantly evaluate its performance and learn to make adjustments in its policy and strategy. In short, winging it and relying on trial-and-error erode a group's chance of success and can be fatal to a movement, while carefully working out its policy, strategy, and tactics improves the group's chances.

Those who believe in Gandhian principles of nonviolence would add the need for faith in God and a deep respect for one's opponent—a desire to transform instead of disarm.

Unable to study nonviolent action in-depth or unaware of the need to develop a strategy, some activists learn as they go. Their course may be haphazard and against the odds, but doing something is usually better than doing nothing at all.

Code of Conduct

Participants of direct actions are often asked to sign pledges of nonviolence or adhere to codes of conduct, which are usually printed on leaflets and distributed at the beginning of an action.

Following is a code of conduct from a blockade of a Trident missile-manufacturing facility that contains rather universal guidelines for principled nonviolent direct actions:[5]

> Our attitude will be one of sincerity and respect toward the people we encounter.
>
> We will not engage in physical violence or verbal abuse toward any individual.
>
> We will carry no weapons.
>
> We will not bring or use any alcohol or drugs other than for medical purposes.
>
> For the purposes of this action, we will assume the destruction of property will not occur.
>
> All participants in the civil disobedience will be organized into affinity groups trained in nonviolence. Affinity groups are expected to notify the organizers of their plans.

Although workshops and nonviolent training sessions offer valuable experience, it can take considerable time to master the skills. Narayan Desai, a lifelong nonviolent activist and disciple of Gandhi, mused that "sixteen years is a good start."[6]

Training notwithstanding, as military troops learn, the real test and the hard lessons occur on the battlefield—during a direct action itself. "Nonviolence is really tough," declared labor leader César Chávez. "You don't practice it by attending conferences . . . you practice it on the picket lines."[7]

Training also comes from family members and the values that one has been taught at home, as Chai Ling, leader of the Chinese students' uprising in Tiananmen Square in 1989 explained: "I was brought up to believe that a principle was worth giving my life for." When the time came for Ling to decide between the principle of freedom and her life, the choice was clear. "I chose to risk my life for freedom," she says.[8]

Even the best-trained nonviolent troops can expect long campaigns and, at times, defeat. Still, no athlete would compete without training; no military troop would engage in battle without training. To achieve success with nonviolence demands the same high standards—the best training a person or group can acquire.

9

In the Line of Duty

It will take all of your courage to walk unarmed and refuse to hate and kill, in a world which insists you must have enemies and be prepared to kill.

—Mairead Corrigan Maguire

Soldiers are willing to risk death to kill the national enemy of the day. We cannot hope to put a stop to injustice if we are not willing to take some personal risks for peace.

—Dan Schechter

In order to succeed against powerful opponents, nonviolent resistance requires the qualities of a warrior—strength, courage, persistence, and refusal to back down in the face of violence or repression. Though many nonviolent sanctions are easy to do and relatively harmless, the most powerful ones ordinarily cause opponents to retaliate in some way. And a lack of discipline can put an entire action at risk of defeat.

We are at a protest in Washington, D.C., in 1986 and the issue concerns United States aid to Contras in Nicaragua, which many people oppose because the Contras are keeping an oppressive regime in power. Two Vietnam veterans vow to fast until they see evidence of a strong protest movement against this United States intervention in Nicaragua. A few weeks later, two more veterans join the protest fast.

Every day this small group of protesters patiently sits on the steps of the Capitol. At first, few people pay attention to them. After a few radio and newspaper interviews, interest in their action mounts. By the sixth week of their fast, dozens of people are joining them each day to sit on the steps and discuss the situation in Nicaragua. Thousands of letters of support also arrive each week.

By now, convinced that their action has successfully focused attention on the issue of Contra aid and inspired many people to join in the protest, the four men end their fast. Yet their commitment to nonviolent protest continues.

Several months later, Vietnam veteran Brian Willson and others organize a vigil outside of California's Concord Naval Weapons station, which is the largest weapons depot on the West Coast. From Concord, weapons are being shipped by train and truck to El Salvador, where they are distributed to United States government–supported troops.

Around the clock, various members of Willson's group hold a vigil beside the train tracks, displaying protest banners. Within weeks, the group plans to blockade the weapons depot to stop weapons from going to Central America. Willson and his colleagues inform the Concord's base commander, the local police, and many United States congresspeople exactly where and why they intend to sit on the tracks and try to stop the munitions train. Word of their action reaches the Pentagon.

On the morning of the blockade, as several reporters stand by, forty protesters gather on the tracks, singing and reading inspirational passages from the Bible and works by Mohandas Gandhi and Martin Luther King Jr.

A letter stating the group's intentions to blockade the transport is delivered to the officer on duty at the gate. Soon afterward, the first train carrying weapons and explosives leaves the gate, pausing on the tracks for several minutes.

Three Vietnam War veterans—Duncan Murphy, David Duncombe, and Brian Willson—sit down on the tracks, in front of the train. Patiently they wait, fully expecting to be removed from the tracks by police and arrested.

Yet no arrests occur. Instead, the train starts moving ahead, flashing its red light and picking up speed. Willson's wife screams to the engineer to stop the train, but the whistle drowns out her pleas. The train picks up more speed.

Sensing trouble, Duncombe rolls off the track and dives for cover. Murphy escapes. Willson tries to get up, too, but the train, moving at three times its normal speed, "smashed into his face, rolling him backward, dragging him under the wheels, breaking his skull, and shredding his legs just below the knees."[1]

Although a naval ambulance is parked nearby, its driver repeatedly refuses to come to Willson's aid. Finally, a civilian ambulance arrives and whisks Willson off to a local hospital. One of his legs was severed by the train; the other must be amputated by doctors.

Critics of Willson's action believe that he was foolish for ever trusting that the train would stop. Others believe that he was courting disaster by planning such a dangerous action in the first place, that he might have done more good for the cause by using other methods.

Paying the Price

Participation in most nonviolent actions and campaigns usually requires little bravery, only time, effort, and commitment. The bulk of nonviolent campaigning involves routine work, such as writing, canvassing, making phone calls, attending meetings, and fund-raising, which require a great deal of time but involve little risk.

Although an illegal demonstration can be dangerous, even for bystanders, most are not. And those people who are unable or unwilling to suffer injury, arrest, or imprisonment can still make significant "behind the scenes" contributions by documenting any arrests or violence, contacting lawyers, and giving other necessary support.

As many nonviolent campaigns have shown, however, putting oneself in the direct line of duty, especially in a leadership role, can bring physical harm, as well as hate mail, bomb threats, and death warnings.

During the Montgomery, Alabama, bus boycott of 1955 to 1956, participants, weary after a long day of manual work, often had to walk miles to get home. Striking workers lose their paychecks and sometimes their jobs. In a few cases, tax resisters have had their cars confiscated, their homes auctioned off, and their bank accounts frozen. Fasters suffer hunger and thirst. Long fasts can permanently impair their health or even kill them. In a repressive political climate, even a simple act like praying, writing a letter to the editor, or giving a speech can have serious consequences.

Of course, a few activists (and occasionally bystanders) pay the ultimate price. At an antiwar protest on May 4, 1970, on a grassy knoll at Kent State University in Ohio, National Guardsmen opened fire on unarmed students, killing four of them and wounding several others. And during the labor movement of the 1930s, thousands of strikers suffered injuries as they picketed and struck for better wages and working conditions.

Some activists purposely risk harming themselves in order to draw attention to a cause or compel their opponent to take action. For example, a month-long prison fast left David Dellinger with a thirty-year case of colitis (a painful digestive condition).

Though many people die for a cause, few commit suicide for one. Such an act is too violent and sacrificial to be considered truly nonviolent. Yet many activists seriously endanger their health or welfare by fasting for long stretches of time, exposing themselves to nuclear fallout during protests at bomb-testing sites, or placing themselves between harpoons and whales. Some causes merit such risks. When the sacrifice reaches beyond what is necessary, though, it becomes martyrdom.

Striking the right balance between a cause and the sacrifice you are willing to make for it is essential. Picketing a school cafeteria because it serves unappetizing food hardly justifies the same risk as picketing a school that refuses to admit minority students.

Many nonviolent theorists believe that the greater the repression and lawlessness by the opponent, the greater should be the suffering of the nonviolent activists fighting them. As Martin Luther King Jr. explained: "My personal trials have taught me the value of unmerited suffering." And he added: "Recognizing the necessity of suffering, I have tried to make it a virtue."[2]

In contrast, other activists know that suffering is unavoidable, but nonetheless fail to see any virtue in it. "Women are already battered, sexually abused, do sixty percent of the world's work and own less than ten percent of the world's wealth," observed one female activist. "This does not mean that women are unwilling to take personal risks, only that they don't see suffering as something valuable *in itself.*"[3]

For the Greater Good

Like any soldier facing combat, Mohandas Gandhi advised participants in nonviolent direct actions "to learn to dare danger and death, mortify the flesh, and acquire the capacity to endure all manner of hardships."[4] Moreover, because they are aware of the risks involved, from lost reputations and arrest to injury and death, many activists have fear as a constant companion. According to Per Herngren, author of a manual on civil disobedience, "the strength of civil disobedience lies in *overcoming the fear* of suffering."[5]

Most activists either learn to overcome their fears or to participate in direct actions anyway, finding it easier to live with their conscience than give in to their fears. "There is the sense of camaraderie with one's fellow activists," explains Anne Shumway of her civil disobedience, "the joy in taking the ultimate risks for what one believes.

"It can also be painful and terrifying, depending on how the police react. But there is usually the satisfaction of knowing that you have taken a giant step in being willing to make a real personal sacrifice for your beliefs. One can say to oneself, 'I have done all I can.' "[6]

Keeping a Stiff Upper Lip

Bearing up to the pain of nonviolent resistance with courage and restraint, and being willing to suffer for a cause serve many purposes:

It can appeal to opponents' good natures and change the way they react to their own violence. According to Gandhian principles, nonviolent activists actually prove their sincerity by their willingness to suffer and their ability to "accept blow after blow, showing no signs of fear or resentment, keeping steadily good-humored, and kindly in look of face, tone of voice, and posture of body and arms."[7] Or, as

Learning to
withstand cruel
treatment gives
activists power.
ELLEN SHUB

F. C. Gartlett observed, "It is easier and requires less courage to attack than to withstand fire without retaliation." An assailent may even lose confidence in himself, as his "brutality becomes more dramatic in contrast to the nonviolence."[8]

One of the most moving examples of this point occurred during a direct action in Bombay, India, in the 1930s. As police rained blow after blow with long, pointed clubs, stoic protesters kept their dignity throughout, refusing to move until they had to be carried away on stretchers.

Reporter Negley Farson, of the Chicago *Daily News,* observed a short, muscular man who took the blows with "ramrod straight posture and dignity, closing his eyes as the blows came." When the man fell to the ground, volunteers wiped the blood that was streaming from his mouth, and brought ice to rub over the lacerations on his eyes. Despite his agony, when reporter Farson glanced over at the man, he smiled and then rose to his feet to take even more blows. Nor was the gentleman alone. All the men participating in the demonstration with him bore their suffering with the same stoicism and dignity.

Finally, the police threw up their hands and refused to attack any more protesters. "You can't go on hitting a blighter when he stands up to you like that," one of them explained.[9]

As long as it is not willful martyrdom, *suffering and dignity can gain public support and garner publicity for a cause.* During the civil rights movement, racist mobs and police brutally assaulted civil rights workers, setting attack dogs on them, hosing them with pressurized water, and dragging them by their hair and limbs. When photographs of this brutality, and the dignity with which the workers stood up to it, reached the public, support for the courageous and dignified civil rights workers grew enormously. At the same time, criticism for those who had inflicted the suffering on the workers mounted.

Remaining calm and refusing to retaliate, despite any pain or injury received, also gives opponents no need to fear or panic, and therefore minimizes the violence that might occur. Nonviolent participants often warn the police of a protest ahead of time, informing them of what to expect from demonstrators. Such warnings lessen the chance of police brutality. Training demonstrators to deal peacefully

Stoicism in the face of brutality can gain considerable public sympathy for a cause.
JIM WEST

with adversity, through role-playing or seeing other actions in person or on film, also improves the chance that an action will remain peaceful. Still, as many nonviolent participants have learned, nothing ensures that an action will not turn violent, especially during large mass protests about highly charged issues.

Weary feet and aching bodies. Fasts and sleepless vigils in all kinds of weather. Hate mail and harassment. Fines, penalties, and property seizure. Bombings, beatings, arrest, and prison. Death. Such risks, particularly the more serious ones, ought to be reserved for important causes. Whether they are saving the environment from massive destruction or ending racial discrimination and segregation, most nonviolent warriors face these risks with dignity and courage.

10

Taking
the Heat

I had a freedom and a power that I didn't realize I had before, that there were things I could do if I were willing to go to jail.

—*Daniel Ellsberg*

Dampness chills the air in front of the White House in January 1917, where several dozen women are silently picketing, carrying banners to reproach President Woodrow Wilson for declaring war "to make the world safe for democracy" while American women are denied the right to vote.

Angry bystanders pelt the women with rotten eggs and tomatoes, blow tobacco smoke in their faces, and shout obscenities at them.

The police do not make a move to control the rowdy crowd. Finally, police reserves appear and within minutes order is restored. However, the police arrest six of the picketers and charge them with obstruction of sidewalk traffic. No one who attacked the women is arrested.

Undaunted, the women continue picketing day after day, even though more and more are arrested and given jail sentences as long as six months.

At the workhouse and jail, where the women are imprisoned,

conditions are deplorable. Some women, such as leader Alice Paul, have been confined to solitary cells. Their mail is censored and sometimes withheld altogether, and for a few weeks the women are allowed no visitors. The meager prison diet consists of disgusting, rancid food.

As their strength deteriorates and conditions remain awful, the women worry about how much more suffering they can endure. To protest their treatment, they embark on the first organized prison fast in United States history.

Just as picketing had brought them woes, fasting now brings new hardship—forced feeding by tube. "We think of the coming feeding all day," lamented prisoner Rose Winslow, "and it is horrible." When she can relax, it is dreadful but tolerable. On other occasions, though, she "vomits continuously," and the tube causes a painful irritation in her throat.[1]

"Never was there a sentence like ours for such an offense as ours. . . ." Winslow observed. "And during all that agitation *we* were busy saying that never would such things happen in the United States."[2]

When word of the prison cruelty leaks to the press, public outrage over it buoys the women's lagging spirits. (It also helps pressure Congress to eventually ratify the Constitutional amendment to give women the vote.) An appeals court throws out the charges against the women and they are released.

Jail has always been one of the prices to pay for nonviolent activism. When Kate Richards O'Hare gave an antiwar speech in North Dakota, she was sentenced to five years in jail. In Tibet, Ama Phurbu-la, a businesswoman from Lhasa, received a three-year prison term for organizing memorial prayers for the victims of a previous demonstration. During India's salt-tax protest, the British arrested more than sixty thousand people. Thousands of people have been arrested for participating in labor strikes, civil rights actions, and antiwar protests. Countless activists fighting for the rights of homosexuals, the disabled, the homeless, animals, or the environment have spent time in jail.

Paying the Price

Accepting the punishment—arrest, conviction, and sentenc-ing—for breaking the law sets civil disobedience apart from ordinary crime because it shows that the person does respect society's laws and is breaking a law for unselfish reasons.

All the same, imprisonment can be harrowing. Most people agree that the first couple of nights are the most trying of their entire experience, unaccustomed as they may be to lack of freedom, confine-ment, sleeping with bright lights, eating unsavory prison food, and using prison latrines.

For many activists, being in prison brings them into fearful proximity to murderers, rapists, and other violent criminals, who some-times inflict violence on them. Nearly one-fourth of the United States inmate population is H.I.V. positive or afflicted with AIDS. Although a few activists find their incarceration tolerable and even an opportu-nity for personal growth, given the dangers of prison today, jail should *never* be romanticized or taken lightly.

In addition to the severity of prison life there is also the risk of unfair sentencing: For causing four hundred and twenty-eight dollars' worth of damage to a nuclear missile warhead in her effort to help stop the nuclear arms race, Jean Gump, wife and mother of twelve, was sentenced to eight years in federal prison.

Making the Best of the Situation

Many activists use their time behind bars to continue their activism, by organizing prison strikes or fasts for better conditions or by using their time to further their own causes.

On April 30, 1977, more than two thousand people illegally occupied a parking lot in Seabrook, New Hampshire, to protest the construction of a nuclear power plant there. Police arrested 1,414 pro-testers. When more than half of the group refused to pay bail, the state of New Hampshire was compelled to hold them for nearly two weeks in National Guard armories.

Jail gave the protesters an opportunity to get to know other people in their campaign. Protesters also took advantage of the time and the togetherness by organizing future direct actions. Finally, their bail solidarity (bail solidarity occurs when a group of people who are jailed act in unison, usually refusing to pay bail) gave them another advantage. Because it was too costly to keep so many people in prison, the state of New Hampshire was compelled to release all the protesters.[3]

Prison can strengthen the morale of people within a movement, as well as inspire others to join it. When Janice Dover visited two peace activists who were serving time in a county jail for their protest action against nuclear weapons, she found their living conditions appalling.

"They had no privacy, no space, no ventilation, no natural light," Dover observed. "The one window, on the visitor's side of the bars, was covered with sheet metal. The men ate, sat, and slept in their bunks, and were taken upstairs for exercise every ten days to two weeks." Despite such trying circumstances, Dover found that the men were "so jovial, optimistic, generous, and loving," and in such good spirits that they strengthened her own commitment to "doing something for the cause of peace." Indeed, that "something" can be a remarkable turning point in a person's life.[4]

In 1969, Daniel Ellsberg, who worked at the United States Department of Defense, was disillusioned with the Vietnam War but felt unable to do anything to stop it. Then he heard Randy Kehler speak about how he deliberately resisted the draft and went to prison. Kehler noted that most of the young men at the forefront of the draft-resistance movement were already in jail.

Ellsberg was moved to tears and inspired to do something himself, risking a 115-year jail sentence to leak top secret information to Arkansas Democratic senator J. William Fulbright and then to the *New York Times.* Releasing the information, later known as *The Pentagon Papers,* did much to turn public opinion against the war. And while Ellsberg was convicted for the act, and did serve time in prison, however terrible his imprisonment was, he never regretted the decision. Today he continues his activism, risking arrest and prison, and credits Kehler and the other imprisoned draft resisters with inspiring him to commit civil disobedience.[5]

Noncooperation

Although the majority of civil disobedients accept jail as the price of their activism, a few nonviolent activists regard the judicial system as so oppressive and unfair that they purposely choose not to cooperate. For stealing and setting fire to hundreds of active draft records to protest the Vietnam War in 1968, Father Daniel Berrigan was sentenced to three years in federal prison, then released until his sentencing began.

Instead of reporting to the federal marshals, Berrigan dodged them for many months, using the time to speak out against the war. Although he knew the decision would be unpopular and misunderstood by many of his own followers, Father Berrigan believed that resisting sentencing was merely a continuation of his protest, especially since he could have left the country instead of going underground and "courting capture."

"My refusal to submit and my refusal to leave the country were, in my mind, both elements of responsibility," explained Father Berrigan. "I couldn't just submit while that war was on, because that would be like being inducted into the war."[6]

Many activists submit to arrest but with little cooperation. At the time of their arrest, they will let their bodies go limp, compelling officers to literally carry them away. Then they will refuse to give their names, social security numbers, and other vital information.

A few activists carry noncooperation even further. Whenever longtime activist Corbin Bishop was sentenced to prison, he would refuse to eat, move himself, or even rise from his cot to tend to his own toilet needs. During one incarceration, his noncooperation was so taxing on prison guards that Bishop's four-year sentence was abruptly terminated in less than a year. Even after Bishop was unconditionally released, he refused to walk out of prison on his own—guards had to carry him to freedom!

Noncooperation is risky business. Activists who go limp at an arrest are often charged with "resisting arrest," which may carry a more severe penalty than what they were arrested for doing. Police officers have to bodily remove them, which can cause physical harm to both protesters and police. Noncooperation through fasting can bring

These people are
willing to be
arrested, but only
with their passive
approval. DOROTHY
MARDER/WAR
RESISTERS' LEAGUE

forced feedings, as well as extremely serious health risks or even death.

Despite the danger of noncooperation, many activists believe it gives them a greater sense of freedom. "The authorities have the power to seize my body," explained Corbin Bishop, "but that is all they can do. My spirit will be free."[7]

Staying out of Jail

Many activists see prison as a necessary part of nonviolent activism. It can even become a mark of honor. For many reasons, however, not all activists agree with this principle. In fact, they believe that too many civil disobedients martyr themselves by being jailed or romanticize the experience. Others feel that a conflict of legitimate interests keeps them from serving on the front line of duty. Parents may feel that serving time in prison imposes too much sacrifice on their children. Or, as a compromise, one parent will refrain from doing civil disobedience in order to take over the responsibilities of the parent who does.

Some nonviolent activists truly believe that they can accomplish their goals without risking prison. During her 1980s campaign to stop the nuclear weapons race, Dr. Helen Caldicott, founder of the group Women's Action for Nuclear Disarmament, continuously advised the mothers in her group that they could stay out of jail and still work hard for the movement.

For his tax resistance, Henry David Thoreau spent only one night in jail and exploited the opportunity to broaden his own horizons by interviewing his cell mate, a man accused of burning down a bar. Thoreau expressed the sentiments of so many protesters who have followed in his footsteps when he wrote, "Under a government which imprisons unjustly, the true place for a just man is also a prison."

Many people disagree with Thoreau's opinion, of course. Moreover, of the approximately one million prisoners currently serving time in the United States, most have been convicted of crimes for which they had intended to avoid punishment. Nevertheless, among the prison population are dozens of idealistic warriors who willingly serve time in order to best serve their country.

3

Nonviolence
at Work

11

Experiment with Truth

Noncooperation with evil is as much a duty as cooperation with good.

—*Mohandas Gandhi*

My noncooperation has its roots not in hatred, but in love.

—*Mohandas Gandhi*

The image of a bald, barefoot man, dressed only in a home-spun cloth, sitting cross-legged and spinning cotton, hardly conjurs up thoughts of great leadership. Yet Mohandas K. Gandhi and his "experiment with truth" led 300 million Indians to overthrow British foreign rule with few casualties in comparison to violent revolutions. In fact, Gandhi created the first large-scale nonviolent movement in history and has inspired hundreds of nonviolent direct actions and movements worldwide.[1]

Little in Gandhi's early background indicated that he would become such a charismatic leader. Born in 1869 to a family from the merchant class, Gandhi grew up in modest circumstances. Keeping with the custom of the day, he married at age thirteen and lived with his parents until he graduated from high school. Then, leaving his wife, Kasturbai, behind, Gandhi went to England to study law.

As soon as he completed his studies, Gandhi returned to India. Unfortunately, he was so shy, speaking in a barely audible tone during his first court appearances, that professional success eluded him. Thus, when Gandhi was invited to work in South Africa, which had a large community of Indian workers, he gladly accepted the offer, unaware that his commitment would stretch into two decades, and that in South Africa he would nearly reinvent himself.

In South Africa, both his family life and legal practice flourished. A quest for moral purity and "right living" that had begun earlier in his life continued. Most of all, Gandhi grew deeply concerned about the injustice he saw; he soon found his calling by fighting for the rights of people, especially the Indians, whom the British grossly mistreated in both South Africa and India.

Drawing on his familiarity with certain Indian traditions, as well as what he learned from extensive reading and correspondence, Gandhi began organizing a new kind of resistance movement. From the Indian tradition of dharna, whereby individuals or small groups fast at the door of an offender in an appeal for justice, Gandhi learned how to use fasting for political ends. The Indian *hartal,* a twenty-four-hour work stoppage, inspired him to use the strike as a nonviolent weapon. Still another Indian tradition—*deshatyaga*—the duty of a wise man to walk away from a corrupt kingdom, taught him how to use tax resistance and boycotts. It was the Hindu tradition of ahimsa, however, and its commitment to nonviolence, respect, and love for all life on earth, that contributed most to Gandhi's nonviolent theory and practice.

With these various traditions, Gandhi put together a unique campaign strategy that was an extraordinary fusion of religion, social action, and politics.

Noncooperation. Gandhi taught his followers "noncooperation," or the refusal to take part in a society that denies basic rights. Participants would refuse to pay taxes or work for a government that denies people the right to vote. Gandhi also implored his followers to take an active stand to correct society's serious problems, even if it meant tackling the problem alone. "History shows that all reforms have begun with one person," Gandhi observed.[2]

Nonviolence. From the Eastern concept of ahimsa, Gandhi advised never using violence against anyone, even if there is reason to believe that they are going to injure or kill. By overcoming a personal fear of injury or death, and learning to accept the suffering, a person gains strength that comes from moral power and not from physical prowess or violent weapons.

Satyagraha. This third principle refers to the ability to find the real truth, to discover what is moral or good about a situation, and then to hold fast to the ideal of nonviolence while resolving a conflict. This means remaining open-minded and willing to understand an opponent's point of view. In this way, both sides (if an opponent is also open-minded) can reach a greater understanding.

Satyagraha also means having compassion and respect for one's enemies, even coming to their aid if necessary. In addition, Gandhi advised seeking to reconcile differences without totally destroying the opponent. For example, he sought to stop British oppression of Indians without stopping the British from living. Finally, satyagraha means letting enemies change without losing face, and being willing to forgive and show mercy, kindness, and love toward them.

Most of all, Gandhi taught that the true power of nonviolence is spiritual, not merely physical, and that it requires faith in God. Nor is satyagraha ever just a mere tactic. For Gandhi, satyagraha offered an entire creed by which to live—as an individual, as a family member, and as part of the human race.

Putting Theory into Practice

In 1906, Gandhi gave satyagraha its first real test when he led a movement to resist certain newly enacted laws, including the requirement that all Indians register with the South African government, submit to fingerprinting, and carry their registration with them at all times, a degrading law that, to Gandhi, "branded them like criminals." Three thousand delegates from the Indian community gathered in Johannesburg to decide how to resist the British and convince them to rescind the oppressive laws. Under Gandhi's leadership, the delegates began a nonviolent campaign.

First, hundreds of Indians publicly burned their registration cards in a huge bonfire. Others picketed the registration office, urging people not to register. Still others defiantly crossed borders without their registration papers. Thousands went on strike against British employers. The British arrested and imprisoned several thousand protesters, including Gandhi.

After eight years of nonviolent campaigning, Britain capitulated to Indian demands and passed the Indian Relief Bill, which revoked many of the unfair laws. Although this first nonviolent campaign proved long and difficult, its success laid the foundation for an even longer, more difficult struggle in Gandhi's native India.

Returning Home

With his remarkable victory in South Africa, Gandhi returned to India as a hero in 1919. Soon he embarked on a full agenda of reform, which included plans to teach 300 million Indians the principles of nonviolence; instruction about healthier, more hygienic living standards; equality for both women and "untouchables" (outcasts from Indian society); and, finally, complete self-rule for India, or swaraj. This broad agenda would dominate the rest of Gandhi's life.

Throughout his leadership during the Indian Nationalist movement, Gandhi fasted many times, led several massive general strikes and boycotts, walked countless miles and visited hundreds of villages, served a total of seven years in jail, and wrote hundreds of essays and articles. One campaign in particular, however, best illustrates Gandhi's deft leadership and political cunning—the Salt March of 1930.

When the Indian National Congress met in December 1929 to resume their drive for self-rule, they turned to Gandhi for guidance, asking him to find a specific focus for their new battle. After two months of contemplation and meditation, Gandhi had a sudden insight: He would lead a march to the sea to make salt. This simple act would blatantly defy the British monopoly on salt production, as well as resist its universal tax on salt.

As usual, Gandhi began the action by making a public announcement of his plan and appealing to British authorities to negotiate an agreement with him. The British refused.

Undaunted, Gandhi set out on the two-hundred-mile trek to the sea on March 12, 1930, with eighty disciples from his ashram (religious community). Carrying a walking stick and garbed in a simple dhoti, or loincloth, the cheerful leader presented quite a picture to the world press, who publicized the march. "We are marching in the name of God," Gandhi explained.

As the band of resisters walked the dirt roads through villages and towns, they were greeted by throngs of supporters, who sprinkled their feet with water and spread leaves and flower petals to soothe their way. By the time the marchers reached the sea town of Dandi, twenty-four days later, their ranks had swelled to thousands.

When they reached the sea, Gandhi ceremoniously waded into the water to bathe and purify himself as members of the international press and throngs of supporters looked on. When he emerged, he stooped and gathered a handful of salt, which had been left by the

Dressed in his usual homespun cloth garb, Mohandas Gandhi marched to the sea in one of his most dramatic and effective protest actions, the Salt March. NATIONAL GANDHI MUSEUM

waves. Like the Boston Tea Party, this one symbolic act of defiance threatened to undermine an entire government. It also inspired hundreds of thousands of Indians to join the protest: Within hours, Indians all over the nation were swarming to the sea to gather salt. Those who were unable to make the pilgrimage to the sea purchased salt from those who could. In this way, millions defied the British salt tax and eroded its monopoly on salt production. Soon, the salt protest spread to boycotts of other British goods, particularly English-woven cloth.

British authorities instructed police to beat protesters with *lathis* (long, metal-tipped sticks) and arrest more than sixty thousand people, including Gandhi himself, whom they sentenced to prison on the charge of sedition against the government.

Despite his imprisonment, his followers decided to go through with his plan to raid the Dharasana Salt Works, one of the British government's salt deposits. Aware of the courage and restraint they would need to bear up to British forces, the twenty-five hundred participants began the protest by praying. Then, in long, straight columns, they solemnly began their protest. As they neared the entrance, they began softly chanting a slogan.

Four hundred police, commanded by six British officials, awaited the protesters. As each line of people advanced, police rushed to attack them. Webb Miller, a correspondent for the United Press, described the horrible scene: "Not one of the marchers even raised an arm to fend off the blows. They went down like tenpins. From where I stood I heard the sickening whacks of the clubs on unprotected skulls. . . . Those struck down fell sprawling, unconscious or writhing in pain with fractured skulls or broken shoulders."[3]

Although the resisters knew that they would be beaten or killed, no one fled from the line or showed fear. Instead, each person marched steadily on, head held high. Even as the police beat them in the abdomens and groins, no one raised an arm to resist or retaliate.

By noon, the heat had reached a scorching 116 degrees Fahrenheit, and the protest ended, leaving more than three hundred injured and two dead.

In August 1947, after nearly three decades of struggle, Britain granted independence to India. But as impressive as Gandhi's nonviolent strategy had been, it had failed to unite the Muslims and Hindus who shared India's destiny. Finally, after extensive rioting, and the death of one million Indians, plus displacement of tens of millions more, India was partitioned into two separate nations—Muslim-dominated Pakistan and Hindu-dominated India.

"My thirty-two years of work have come to an inglorious end," lamented Gandhi. Months later, a Hindu fanatic shot the beloved leader as he was strolling through a garden on his way to address a crowd of admirers.

Despite the years he had spent in jail and the major setbacks that had occurred, Gandhi refused to accept defeat. He realized that nonviolence requires time, patience, and tenacity to succeed. As Gandhi said, "Nonviolence is a plant of slow growth. It grows imperceptibly, but surely."[4]

12

In
Self-defense

In principle, people committed to nonviolence do not carry weapons. It is because we believe in ahimsa, but it is also because we believe that in a crisis our personal ability is more effective than a gun.

—*Gerard A. Vanderhaar*

On October 17, 1992, Webb Haymaker and Yoshihiro Hattori, the Japanese exchange student staying with him, drove to a Halloween party in Baton Rouge, Louisiana. Haymaker, who had to wear a neck brace because of a diving injury, was costumed as an accident victim, with his head wrapped in an Ace bandage that left only his face visible. Hattori, who loved to dance, had donned a white dinner jacket to look like John Travolta in the movie *Saturday Night Fever.*

The boys arrived at the wrong house. The owners of the house, Bonnie and Rodney Peairs, felt seriously threatened. It was two weeks before Halloween, they had recently been robbed, and the boys looked rather bizarre in their costumes. Aware that he had a legal right to use a gun to defend his home and family against a break-in, Rodney Peairs crouched in his driveway and aimed a 44-caliber gun at Hattori.

"Freeze!" Peairs yelled to the two boys.

Hattori, who spoke broken English, probably didn't understand the word *freeze.* He started skipping up the driveway. "I'm here for the party," he giddily sang out. "I'm here for the party!"[1]

Even if he noticed the pistol that Peairs was pointing at him, Hattori probably thought it was a Halloween prop.

Wrong house, misunderstandings, mistaken threats. When Hattori was halfway up the driveway, Peairs panicked and pulled the trigger, shooting Hattori in the chest and killing him.

Louisiana law gave Rodney Peairs the right to defend himself with violence. After an emotionally wrenching trial, Peairs was acquitted of any crime. For many, Peairs had the moral right to defend himself against the threat of crime, especially since he had been victimized by a break-in only a short time before the incident.

Yet even when we have the legal and moral right to defend ourselves by using violent methods, Hattori's tragic death reminds us that alternative methods can spare us similar tragedies. Nonviolence can also, in some circumstances, actually protect people from harm. Take John Cady, for example.[2] When the retired minister heard his back door being jimmied open by an apparent robber, Cady, who is deeply committed to nonviolence, opened the door and calmly said, "If you need something that badly, just ask." Then, with a handshake, he introduced himself. "Now, how can I help you?"[3]

No doubt startled by such friendliness and fearlessness, the young intruder simply muttered an apology and ran off.

Instead of acting unexpectedly friendly, Margaret Teewood handled her situation differently. As she was leaning on her car, several menacing-looking gang members approached her and began rocking it. Knowing that she could not outrun them and aware that she was outnumbered and no one might come to her aid, Teewood serenely climbed on the hood of her car and deliberately dropped her car keys down the front of her dress. Surprised at her fearless, unconventional response to the danger facing her, the gang members walked away, leaving Teewood unscathed and able to drive away to safety.[4]

Whether to use violent or nonviolent methods to defend yourself from personal attack is an exceedingly difficult decision—one that can, in certain circumstances, mean the difference between life and death. If an attacker is psychotic (mentally out of touch with reality), high on drugs, or too drunk to reason or feel guilt, then non-violence may not work at all. It may also fail against criminally hardened or determined assailants.

Some principled nonviolent activists would rather die than use violence to defend either themselves or anyone else. Others, committed to nonviolent social action, would not hesitate to use violence, at least as a last resort. After she was raped, Adele Stan decided that using violence was a right accorded to anyone threatened by violence. In fact, it proved liberating to her. "I have been grabbed several times by strangers on the street," she explains, "and I never let the culprit go without physically attacking him. When a vile remark is shouted at me, I shout back something equally vile." According to Stan, young women should be taught to be violent toward attackers. "If there really is a war against women," reasons Stan, "then we ought to be raising women warriors."[5]

Right or wrong aside, there is a practical issue here: In certain circumstances, nonviolent methods can actually be more effective than violent methods.

It is important to remember, however, that while nonviolent self-defense can broaden your range of options, and perhaps give you superior ones, it cannot always ensure safety from harm. On the other hand, neither does violence. Americans possess more than 200 million guns, yet we have the highest crime rate of any industrialized nation.[6] And using a weapon in self-defense can cause a situation to worsen or, as Rodney Peairs learned, inflict harm on the harmless.

Common Sense and Presence of Mind

Like nonviolent social and political action, nonviolent self-defense is not passive. It is never as simple as turning your cheek to harm or willingly accepting that you will be victimized. Instead, nonviolent self-defense requires taking an *active* part in your self-defense and substituting mental and emotional resources for violence. It requires a clear, calm mind, as well as the courage to refuse to act fearful or powerless.

Reliance on nonviolent tactics should never be a substitute

for common sense and an effort to avoid or escape danger in the first place. You need to learn to be aware of danger and to spot it when you still have an easy opportunity to escape. Nor do nonviolent principles imply trust in all people. As feminist Mary Crane advises, "Our belief in nonviolence does not mean that we have to constantly trust men or believe that they are always well-intentioned toward us. We can both respect and cherish the humanity of all men, while at the same time maintaining a healthy self-protectiveness against possible male assaults."[7] And as African-American civil rights workers used to say during their struggle, "We love our white brothers, but we don't trust them."[8]

Like nonviolent social and political action, nonviolent self-defense relies on the ability to surprise an assailant with unconventional behavior. This surprise may simply be a refusal to act like a "typical" victim—fearful, submissive, or passive. Or it may come, as the earlier examples in this chapter show, by going further and surprising assailants with compassion and respect, even when you don't think they "deserve" such respect or compassion. Mostly, though, the strength of nonviolent self-defense comes from convincing yourself that you have the power not to be victimized.

Sally Donaldson and her two children found themselves stranded on the turnpike late one night. When Sally looked up, she saw a man brandishing a gun through her window, ordering her to let him in the car.

Rather than panic, Donaldson looked him straight in the eye and commanded him to "put that gun away and get in your own car and push me to the service area. And," she emphasized, *"I mean right now!"*[9]

No doubt her assailant was surprised by her response, for he did as she had told him: He put his gun away, got in his car, and pushed her car to the service station, then left.

Not only had Donaldson refused to act like a victim, but she also treated the stranger as though he meant no harm, appealing to his better nature. It is important to remember that such tactics can backfire and that he could have pushed her to a lonely area rather than the service station. Further, if he had been mentally unstable or on drugs or alcohol, trying to reason with him also could have resulted in failure. Nevertheless, the situation illustrates the important principle of nonviolent self-defense: Refuse to act like a victim and your assailant may decide not to victimize you, after all. Like other nonviolent situations, treating an assailant as a human being offers the chance, however remote, that you will evoke a sense of decency in him and that his conscience will not allow him to harm you.

A Few Guidelines

From the Peace Grows course on nonviolence, "Alternatives to Violence," Mark Morris of the War Resisters League offers this basic plan for nonviolent self-defense if you are directly confronted by a would-be assailant:[10]

Be clear and reasonable about your own objectives. You may decide during an attempted assault, for example, that you are willing to let your would-be assailant rob but not physically assault you.

Try to overcome your fear or at least hide it. Breathe deeply, talk slowly and in a deep voice, and try to maintain eye contact. Focusing on your assailant and encouraging him or her to talk can help you overcome your fear. Concentrating on what you intend to do once the assault has ended or memorizing details of your assailant's appearance can also help you maintain your presence of mind.

Before you ever face a threatening situation, rehearse what you might do or say. Make up scenarios in your mind—of a deserted parking lot and your home, for instance—and practice what you would say to someone. Remember, because each situation is different, it is impossible to prepare for one before it occurs. Still, rehearsing can bolster courage and help you stay calm and quick-witted.

Try not to frighten your assailant. As ridiculous as it may seem, your assailant may be as scared of committing a crime as you are of being the victim of one. Therefore, always try to move slowly and deliberately. When practical, warn the person ahead of time of what you are going to do. Refrain from saying anything threatening, critical, or hostile, or making sudden gestures, such as reaching into your pocket, which could be misconstrued as reaching for a weapon.

State the obvious. If your assailant grabs your arms, for instance, don't hesitate to calmly tell him or her that it hurts.

Avoid behaving like a victim. Especially if they have committed crimes before, assailants usually have strong expectations of how their victims will or should behave. If you act differently from that expectation—neither threatening, fearful, nor passive, for example—then perhaps you can surprise an assailant into abandoning any plans to harm you.

If possible, try to befriend your opponent's "better nature." Many people, however horrific their behavior, perceive themselves as basically decent. If you can find this spark of decency, perhaps by asking an assailant questions about his or her own life or by demonstrating that you have compassion or concern for his or her safety, you may be able to persuade the person not to harm you.

Respond to physical violence assertively. The traditional response to physical attack is to fight back, flee, or passively sit down, maybe curl up in a fetal position. Another alternative, though, is to resist attack as creatively and as assertively as you can, short of using physical violence. For example, one woman threw her assailant off guard by singing and dancing and spiraling away from him.

Keep talking and keep listening. Encourage your assailant to talk to you, about his or her beliefs, wishes, fears, childhood, or other personal subjects. Never argue with your opponent, but don't give the impression that you agree with anything the assailant says that is cruel or immoral. Remember, too, that actively listening is more important than anything you say.

To fight crime nonviolently, some demonstrators choose a night when hordes of people literally "take back the streets" from criminals. Other citizens band together to patrol their neighborhoods, organize against drug dealing and street crime, and provide shelters for people who are victimized by domestic crime, such as battered women and abused children.

Nonviolent defense requires enormous energy and courage. It does not always work and it is rarely easy. Personal violence is often a response to institutionalized violence, such as poverty, racism,

Each year,
students on
college campuses
participate in a
Take Back the
Night demonstra-
tion, where they
protest crime and
assert their right
to safety.
ELLEN SHUB

and political oppression. Until we find alternatives to the violence on the larger scale of human affairs, people may never be convinced that it can work on a personal level. Still, more and more people are discovering the power of *active* nonviolence.

13

Farewell
to Arms

*When I see people picking up arms when they have
no other alternative, I do not condemn them. But I know
that when they do so, it is another excuse that our military
and the powerful in our country [Guatemala] have to smash
them. The power of nonviolence has to be learned by the
majority of people.*

—*Julio Quan*

*Nonviolent civilian defense is truly the strength of the
citizen and the power of the people.*

—*Jean-Marie Muller*

It is hard to believe that peace can be achieved without
war. Nor is it conceivable to maintain national security without a
standing army or a deep arsenal of sophisticated weaponry.

Yet without a military force, Czechs managed to stave off
Soviet armed forces for eight months, unarmed German citizens tore
down the Berlin Wall and reunited their nation, and Polish citizens
dismantled communism.

Back in 1948, the tiny Central American country of Costa Rica
disbanded its small military. Army barracks were converted into a
cultural center, while the funds previously designated for the army went
to education. Rodrigo Carazo Odio, former president of Costa Rica,
observed, "A country that organizes an army becomes its own jailer."[1]

Although Costa Rica receives military aid from the United
States and maintains a well-trained police force, it still has no standing
army and no intention of establishing one. Moreover, despite being
surrounded by nations where war is no stranger, Costa Rica maintains
both its neutrality and peace within its borders, as well as the highest
standard of living in Central America.[2]

Armies of Peace

In 1910, the American philosopher William James analyzed the growing militarism in Europe and the "raw emotional appeal of war."[3] James observed that the military serves an important function in society: It teaches young people essential values, such as self-discipline, obedience, "purposeful poverty" (how to live with few possessions), noble sacrifice, courage, and patriotism—in general, a "hardihood of character."[4]

To provide an alternative to the military as a moral "training ground," James suggested establishing a different kind of army, one that could cultivate many of the same values. This "moral equivalent to war," as James called his army prototype, would draft young people into several years of service. Instead of learning how to prepare for war, they would direct their energies toward fighting natural disasters and social ills. In this way, the new army would foster character development without destroying any life or property.

Because he drafted his proposal in the midst of industrialization, widespread poverty, and social injustice, James recommended an agenda of road building, mining, laying railroad tracks, and other projects that required hard labor. This ensured that even young people destined to go into white-collar jobs could learn to empathize with people who did hard physical labor.

Though the basic idea for a peace army remains untried by any nation, it has inspired several "armies of peace," and is similar to organizations such as the Peace Corps and Vista. One such army was founded by Gandhi in 1922. Called the Shanti Sena, Gandhi's peace army relied exclusively on nonviolent tactics to try to stem the growing violence between Muslims and Hindus in India.

In 1962, three renowned pacifists, A.J. Muste, Jayaprakash Narayan, and Michael Scott, established a peace army based on nonviolent principles, called the World Peace Brigade. During its brief existence, Brigade volunteers used nonviolent tactics to aid in the Zambian independence movement, intercede during a Chinese-Indian border conflict, intervene in nuclear-weapons testing, and carry out other reconciliation work.

More recently, in 1981, a group met in Toronto, Canada, to

form Peace Brigades International (PBI). Attracting volunteers from dozens of nations, PBI trains people to be unarmed bodyguards, non-violent educators, and mediators in violence-torn areas of the world, such as Central America and Burma.

How could an unarmed woman, such as Deborah Rivkin from Chicago, protect Rigoberta Menchú, Guatemalan rights activist and winner of the Nobel Peace Prize, who is unable to walk alone in Guatemala City without risk of being assassinated? Like other trained PBI volunteers, Rivkin guards Menchú by witnessing any wrongdoing or threats to Menchú, and reporting them to the international press. Rivkin can also contact a network of international volunteers.

When both the daughter and the niece of Raquel Portilla, leader of the Salvadoran Woman's Association, were taken hostage in El Salvador, for example, a PBI guard who witnessed the kidnapping alerted both the press and a network of volunteers outside El Salvador. After members of the network sent hundreds of telegrams to the commander in charge of the kidnapping, he released his young hostages.

"No one knows how many deaths and disappearances PBI has prevented," observes Dieter Overath of Amnesty International, a group that monitors political prisoners, "but in a way that's the good part: They can work preventively, keep some of the bad things from happening."[5]

Peace Brigades volunteers also mediate disputes and teach nonviolent methods to groups in conflict. In 1989, for instance, Peace Brigades volunteers went to Sri Lanka to mediate the return of thousands of people who had disappeared. In addition, they brought Sinhalese and Tamil leaders together in retreats, where they helped the warring parties work together on peaceful solutions to their conflicts.

Defending a Nation

Although peace armies do valuable work, they are too small to have a significant influence on international affairs or to stop most of the violence in the world. A few experts, however, including political scientist and international consultant Gene Sharp, believe that it is possible for citizens to use nonviolent methods and strategies on a large scale to defend themselves against military invasion or internal takeovers. In this way, ordinary people could assume responsibility for their own defense and limit their reliance on the military.

In nonviolent defense, ordinary citizens use nonviolent sanctions to defend themselves against foreign invasions or internal takeovers. They may do it on their own (civilian-based defense) or with the military (social defense).

According to Sharp, the key to understanding nonviolent defense is to understand that *the power to rule comes from consent.* Out of fear, respect, habit, or indifference, a populace *consents* to be ruled. If they withdraw that consent entirely, they are no longer governable.[6]

The first modern example of nonviolent resistance occurred in nineteenth-century Hungary, when Austrian emperor Franz Josef ordered an invasion of Hungary. As the Austrian army marched through Hungary, many Hungarians felt helpless to prevent the Austrian occupation.

Ferenc Deák, a Hungarian landowner, implored his fellow Hungarians to refuse to consent to be ruled. "Your laws are violated," Deák admonished, "yet your mouths remain closed. Woe to

When millions of Soviet citizens publicly demonstrated against their communist government, their withdrawal of consent paved the way for a new, democratic government rule.
ROGER S. POWERS

the nation that raises no protest when its rights are outraged. It contributes to its own slavery by its silence. The nation that submits to injustice and oppression without protest is doomed."[7]

With Deák's inspiration and leadership, the Hungarians began a clever strategy of noncooperation against their Austrian invaders. The Hungarian populace boycotted all Austrian goods, declined to serve in the Austrian army, and refused to pay anything to the Austrian tax collectors.

After Austrian police seized Hungarian goods for tax nonpayment, not a single Hungarian auctioneer would sell off the confiscated goods. When an Austrian auctioneer assumed the task, he could find no bidders.

In time, Austria's confidence about ruling Hungary eroded, and on February 18, 1867, Austria restored self-rule to Hungary.

Even when a nonviolent strategy is less effective, it can still empower a populace. In 1969, after the United States government closed a federal prison on Alcatraz Island, in San Francisco Bay, a group of seventy-eight Native Americans, calling themselves Indians of All Tribes, occupied the abandoned prison.[8] After renaming the area Indian Land, they announced their grievances and demanded that the prison be converted into a Native American cultural and educational center.

Soon others from around the nation joined them in their protest. Despite shortages of food, water, heat, and electricity, the occupation lasted over one and a half years. Then, at gunpoint, federal marshals removed the few protesters who remained.

Although the occupation failed to secure the island, it successfully publicized the group's grievances. Furthermore, it bolstered the morale of Native Americans and inspired many others to take on the cause of Native American rights.

Putting an Idea to Work

For the most part, nonviolent resistance has occurred only spontaneously. An entire population has never been trained to do nonviolent action or had a detailed nonviolent strategy of civilian-based defense. Thus, nonviolent defense largely remains untried and theoretical. (By 1995, however, several small nations, including Latvia, Lithuania, Estonia, and Sweden, all of which have limited military strength, had considered adopting some form of nonviolent defense into their overall defense schemes.)

Imagine the power of people to defend their nation if they trained and prepared for a long, widespread, nonviolent defense before they needed to use it. Imagine, too, the power of citizens who work together *with their military* to use nonviolent sanctions instead of military power.

Even if civilians fail to achieve total victory, nonviolent defense ensures them more control over their own lives. For that reason alone, nonviolent defense deserves attention. And when we think of the heavy toll the international community always pays for violence, we can see that nonviolent defense merits strong consideration.

CHAPTER

14

Against
All Odds

People try nonviolence for a week, and when it doesn't work, they go back to violence, which hasn't worked for centuries.

—*Theodore Roszak*

Gallaudet College in Washington, D.C., is unique for being the country's only liberal arts college for the deaf. Yet in Gallaudet's entire 124-year history, deaf people had little say in how to run the school. Few deaf people sat on the board of trustees and not a single one of the university's presidents had ever been deaf.

In 1988, the trustees appointed another hearing person, Dr. Elisabeth Ann Zinser (who didn't even know sign language), to fill the position of president. Angered at such hypocrisy, Gallaudet students went on strike and took over the administration building.

Within hours, Gallaudet's faculty members and alumni joined the student protest, and several consumer groups, labor unions, and politicians lent their support as well. Protesters burned effigies of Zinser, while deaf students from across the country showed their solidarity by writing letters and traveling to Gallaudet for the protest.[1]

By week's end, Dr. Zinser had resigned, and the board of trustees replaced her with Gallaudet's dean of student affairs, I. King Jordan, who is deaf. In addition, they promised to add more deaf people to the board.

When students at Gallaudet College protested in order to have a deaf person appointed president of their school, they gained great public support.
RICK REINHARD

In a way, both sides of the Gallaudet conflict emerged a winner. Dr. Zinser was pressured to resign, but the appointment of deaf persons to both the presidency and trusteeship brought not only justice to the protesters but also goodwill to a university claiming sensitivity to the deaf community.

Most conflicts are not resolved with such a positive balance. More often, one side gives in because it is in their best interest to end the confrontation or because they have no other choice.

Sometimes, a victory is overlooked. When nearly a million students and other Chinese citizens took over Tiananmen Square in Beijing, in June 1989, to protest for a more democratic government, they held off the Chinese government's 38th Army Division for days. They stated their demands, garnered worldwide publicity, legitimacy, and support, and had a victory on their hands. Had they recognized that victory and retreated from the square before the army massacred so many of them, they might have gained the chance to continue their struggle uninterrupted.

Some groups quit too early in a battle to claim a victory. Or they measure their strength on just one or two failed actions, instead of viewing their struggle from a larger perspective. Although some nonviolent contests end quickly, many require a long-term commitment. Greenpeace activists worked for more than a decade to curtail whaling. Gandhi's nonviolent campaign for Indian independence took more than thirty years to achieve. As these examples show, it is important not to surrender to defeat too early in the struggle.

Other groups "put too many eggs in one basket" or expect immediate success. Instead of concentrating their energies on one or two actions, they might have more staying power if they planned smaller, more frequent actions and measured their success in progressive steps. For example, a group planning a large demonstration to stop a toxic-waste plant from operating in its community might be better off starting with a small protest to demand a meeting with one of the company's officials. At the same time, the group could do door-to-

During the student protest in Beijing, China, the tent city students constructed during the demonstrations showed solidarity, even in the face of eventual defeat.
BRUCE JENKINS

door canvassing, pass out leaflets, and collect signatures for petitions to build broad support for its cause. Eventually the group could plan larger actions.

But nonviolence offers no insurance against setbacks or defeat. Some people, especially those fighting huge, powerful opponents, wonder if their efforts make any lasting mark. But they keep fighting anyway, because to stop fighting means even greater defeat. Indeed, finding the courage and resolve to fight nonviolently at all is a victory of sorts. As one activist explained of an antiwar protest that failed, "If the experiment now seems not to have succeeded, that is not to say that . . . it wasn't worth trying."[2] And when Martin Luther King Jr. was asked if his civil disobedience was either efficient or politically shrewd, King replied that neither was the point. To him, the true issue was, "Is it right or wrong?"[3]

Naturally, a judgment call is easier to make from the armchair of history than from the trenches of the battlefield. However, defeat can serve a great purpose if activists learn from their mistakes and apply their hindsight to future strategies.

Conflict is unavoidable and even necessary. But how we deal with conflict is our choice. When the conflict has escalated to the point of war or genocide, it often feels that there is little choice but to stop violence with violence. Fortunately, most of our conflicts and struggles never reach such tragic depths. Yet many people still choose to fight violently or use whatever power they have to destroy their enemies completely. Others turn an indifferent cheek and avoid fighting altogether. Steadily, though, a call to action and to people power is gaining a foothold and making history in new ways.

From the dramatic overthrow of communism in Poland and other east European nations to the end of apartheid in South Africa, from the rescue of thousands of whales and dolphins from yearly slaughter to passage of the American Disabilities Rights Act, from the victories of the suffrage, civil rights, and labor movements to all the other lesser triumphs—time and again, people power has proven its strength.

The dream of many nonviolent activists, particularly those

who are committed to nonviolent principles as a way of life, is to make the world a better place—not only better but truly decent, a concept in Judaism called *tikun olam,* which means "to make the world whole." What matters is not whether such a dream is possible but whether the dream can inspire us to *act as if it were.*

We can use people power to improve our lives, little by little. And as some of the people-powered victories prove, even those that were spontaneous, unplanned, and limited in their success, nonviolence can help us take giant steps toward attaining our dream of a just society and a peaceful planet. Indeed, nonviolent methods give ordinary people the ability to take on the world's Goliaths—and sometimes succeed.

Time and again, nonviolence gives ordinary people the power to bring about extraordinary change. RICK REINHARD

Endnotes

CHAPTER **1** Taking on Goliath

1. Annette Miller et al., "Do Boycotts Work?" *Newsweek* (6 July 1992), p. 58.
2. Gene Sharp, "The Power and Potential of Nonviolent Struggle," *Nonviolent Sanctions* (Spring/Summer 1990), p. 3.
3. Gerard A. Vanderhaar and Mary Lou Kownacki, eds., *Way of Peace* (Erie, Pa.: Pax Christi, 1987), p. 83.
4. Verna Spaethe, "Organizing for Disability Rights," *Peace and Justice Journal* (Winter 1992), p. 6.
5. Quoted in Robert Cooney and Helen Michalowski, eds., *The Power of the People* (Philadelphia: New Society, 1987), pp. 178–79.
6. Mubarak E. Awak, "Non-violent Resistance," *Journal of Palestine Studies* (Summer 1984), p. 23.
7. Souad Dajani, "The Intifada: Nonviolent Struggle in the Middle East," *Nonviolent Sanctions* (Spring/Summer 1990), p. 7.
8. David McReynolds, "Pacifism in Time of War," leaflet (New York: War Resisters League, 1993), p. 1.

CHAPTER **2** Playing by the Rules

1. Quoted in Jenny Labalme, *A Road to Walk* (Durham, N.C.: The Regulator Press, 1987), p. 5.
2. Chris Cook, "Nonviolent Struggle in International Social Movements," *Nonviolent Sanctions* (Spring/Summer 1990), p. 18.
3. Christopher Kruegler, "Gandhi, Clausewitz, and the 'New World Order,'" *Nonviolent Sanctions* (Spring/Summer 1992), pp. 5–6.

CHAPTER **3** People Power

1. "Out in the Backroom," *The Disability Rag* (July 1984), p. 4.
2. "Capitol Steps Climbed in Protest by Disabled," Associated Press Wire Service (13 March 1990).
3. Gene Sharp, *The Methods of Nonviolent Action,* vol. 2 (Boston: Porter Sargent, 1973).
4. Susan Nelson, "Tax Day Actions Tell It Like It Is—You Can, Too," *Conscience* (Spring 1991), p. 4.
5. Michael Brown and John May, *The Greenpeace Story* (New York: Dorling Kindersley, 1991), p. 135.

CHAPTER **4** Mark of Distinction

1. Quoted in Cooney and Michalowski, eds., *The Power of the People,* p. 115.
2. Quoted in Ibid., p. 155.
3. Martin Luther King Jr., "Nonviolence and Racial Justice," *The Christian Century* (6 February 1957), p. 166; cited in John J. Ansbro, *Martin Luther King, Jr.* (Maryknoll, N.Y.: Orbis Books, 1984), p. 9.
4. David Dellinger, *From Yale to Jail* (New York: Pantheon Books, 1993), p. 89.
5. Quoted in *The Power of the People,* p. 139.
6. According to David Barash, both the South African bushmen (or San) and the Eskimo have never engaged in war. Granted, this may be because they have never had to defend themselves or have never been able to defend themselves against aggressors. See David P. Barash, *Introduction to Peace Studies* (Belmont, Calif.: Wadsworth Publishing, 1991), pp. 144–45.
7. Martin Luther King Jr., "Pilgrimage to Nonviolence," reprinted in McCarthy, ed., *Alternatives to Violence,* p. 78. Martin Luther King Jr. often quoted Booker T. Washington on this subject.
8. Richard B. Gregg, *The Power of Nonviolence* (New York: Schocken Books, 1966), chapters 1 and 2 (pp. 15–51).

CHAPTER **5** Breaking the Law to Change the Law

1. Kathy Boylan, "Writings from Jail," *The Nuclear Resister* (23 June 1993), p. 4.
2. Martin Luther King Jr., "Letter from Birmingham Jail," reprinted in Robert L. Holmes, ed., *Nonviolence in Theory and Practice* (Belmont, Calif.: Wadsworth Publishing, 1990), p. 71.
3. Mark Sommer, "Paying the Price for an Act of Conscience," *The Christian Science Monitor* (23 March 1992), p. 18.
4. Jerry Schwartz, "Leaders of Abortion Protest Are Jailed after Refusing to Pay $1000 Fine," *New York Times* (6 October 1989).
5. "Taxing Conscience," *The Nuclear Resister* (7 May 1992), p. 3.

CHAPTER **6** For Appearance's Sake

1. Terri Salvatore, "Jail Releases Protestors," *The Enterprise* (Dobbs Ferry), (8 February 1991), p. 3.
2. Joan M. Mazzolini, "Anti-abortion Activists Take Aim at Doctors," *Cleveland Plain Dealer* (14 July 1993), p. 8.

CHAPTER **7** When Might Makes Right

1. Robert F. Williams, *Negroes with Guns* (Chicago: Third World Press, 1962), p. 10.
2. Quoted in Ibid., p. 43.
3. Ibid., p. 10.

4. Ibid., p. 121.

5. Quoted in Ibid., p. 26.

6. Devi Prasad, *Gandhi on Violent Struggles,* A.J. Muste Memorial Institute Essay Series, pamphlet no. 8.

7. Daniel Berrigan, "Letter to Ernesto Cardenal," reprinted in McCarthy, ed., *Alternatives to Violence,* p. 148.

8. Ibid., p. 149.

9. Ibid.

10. Joan Baez, from *Daybreak,* reprinted in John H. Yoder, *What Would You Do?* (Scottsdale, Pa.: Herald Press, 1983), p. 68.

11. Martin Buber, "A Letter to Gandhi (1939)," reprinted in Doris Hunter and Krishna Mallick, eds., *Nonviolence Reader* (New York: University Press of America, 1990), pp. 139–147; Amy Singer, "Gandhi and the Jews," *Reform Judaism* (Winter 1984–85), p. 6.

12. Ibid., p. 147.

13. Peter Ackerman, "Strategic Aspects of Nonviolence Resistance Movements" (Ph.D. diss., Tufts University, 1976).

14. Barash, *Introduction to Peace Studies,* pp. 446–49.

15. Michael Walzer, *Just and Unjust Wars* (New York: Basic Books, 1977).

CHAPTER **8** Learning the Way of the Warrior

1. Grace Hedemann, "Nonviolence Training," *War Resisters League Organizer's Manual* (New York: War Resisters League, no date), pp. 170–75.

2. Ibid.

3. Cooney and Michalowski, eds., *The Power of the People,* p. 153.

4. Peter Ackerman and Christopher Kruegler, *Strategic Nonviolent Conflict* (Westport, Conn.: Praeger, 1994), p. 2.

5. Leaflet, undated, from the papers of Swarthmore College Peace Collection at Swarthmore College, Swarthmore, Pennsylvania.

6. Quoted in *Nonviolence Training: A Directory of Resource People* (New York: War Resisters League, no date).

7. Quoted in Jeanne Larson and Madge Micheels-Cyrus, *Seeds of Peace* (Philadelphia: New Society, 1987), p. 174.

8. Chai Ling, "A Road to Freedom" (speech), Hudson, Ohio, 19 October 1993.

CHAPTER **9** In the Line of Duty

1. Fred A. Wilcox, *Uncommon Martyrs* (New York: Addison-Wesley, 1991), p. 136.

2. Martin Luther King Jr., *Strength to Love* (Philadelphia: Fortress Press, 1963), p. 35.

3. Feminism and Nonviolence Study Group, *Piecing It Together: Feminism and Nonviolence* (London: War Resisters League, 1983), pp. 30–35.

4. Mohandas K. Gandhi, *The Moral and Political Writings of Mohandas Gandhi,* ed. by Ragharan Iyer, vol. 2 (1986) and vol. 3 (1987), (New York: Oxford University Press), reprinted in Holmes, ed., *Nonviolence in Theory and Practice,* p. 55.

5. Per Herngren, *Path of Resistance* (Philadelphia: New Society, 1993), p. 136.

6. Feminism and Nonviolence Study Group, *Piecing It Together: Feminism and Nonviolence,* pp. 30–35.

7. Quoted in R.R. Diwakar, *Satyagraha: The Power of Truth* (Hinsdale, Ill.: Henry Regnery Co., 1948), p. 70.

8. This change is referred to as "moral jujitsu" and is described clearly in Richard B. Gregg, *The Power of Nonviolence* (New York: Schocken Books, 1966), chapters 2 and 3 (pages 43–59).

9. Quoted in Diwakar, *Satyagraha,* p. 73.

CHAPTER **10** Taking the Heat

1. Quoted in Doris Stevens, *Jailed for Freedom* (New York: Boni and Liveright, 1920), p. 169.
2. Ibid., p. 190.
3. Ed Hedemann, *War Tax Resistance,* 4th ed. (Philadelphia: New Society, 1992), p. 226.
4. Quoted in Samuel H. Day, ed., *Prisoners on Purpose: A Peacemaker's Guide to Jails and Prisons* (Madison, Wis.: A Nukewatch Book, The Progressive Foundation, 1989), p. 95.
5. Wesley Blit, "Ellsberg Credits Kehler with Inspiration," Franklin *Union-News,* 2 March 1992, pp. 1 and 4.
6. Quoted in Wilcox, *Uncommon Martyrs,* p. 39.
7. Quoted in Cooney and Michalowski, eds., *The Power of the People,* pp. 407–8.

CHAPTER **11** Experiment with Truth

1. There are many fine books about Mohandas Gandhi, as well as numerous volumes of his own writings. For a brief overview of his life, however, see the film *Gandhi,* directed by Richard Attenborough (1982; available on video).
2. Reprinted in Holmes, ed., *Nonviolence in Theory and Practice,* p. 53.
3. Webb Miller, "Dharasana Salt Raid," reprinted in *The Gandhi Reader,* ed. Homer A. Jack (Bloomington, Ind.: Indiana University Press, 1956), pp. 248–53.
4. Quoted in Jeanne Larson and Madge Micheels-Cyrus, *Seeds of Peace* (Philadelphia: New Society Publishers, 1987), p. 168.

CHAPTER **12** In Self-defense

1. Joe Treen, Ron Ridenour, and Kimberly Aylward, "Death of a Visitor," *People* (11 November 1992), p. 78.
2. The names of people in this and several other incidents in this chapter have been changed.
3. Gerard A. Vanderhaar, *Active Nonviolence—A Way of Personal Peace* (Mystic, Conn.: Twenty-Third, 1990), p. 76.
4. Gerard A. Vanderhaar, "Nonviolent Response to Assault," reprinted in McCarthy, ed., *Alternatives to Violence,* p. 9.
5. Adele M. Stan, "Women Warriors," *New York Times,* 17 December 1993.
6. U.S. Bureau of Alcohol, Tobacco, and Firearms, reported in Erik Eckholm, "Ailing Gun Industry Confronts Outrage Over Glut of Violence," *New York Times,* 8 March 1992.
7. Mary Crane, "Rape Avoidance and Resistance: A Non-Violent Approach," *WIN Magazine* (26 April 1979).
8. Quoted in Williams, *Negroes with Guns,* p. 16.
9. Vanderhaar, "Nonviolent Response," p. 10.
10. Mark Morris, "Nonviolent Self-defense," reprinted in John Looney, ed., *Alternatives to Violence Workbook* (Akron, Ohio: Peace Grows, 1991), pp. 61–5.

CHAPTER **13** Farewell to Arms

1. Quoted in Susan Steinberg, "Costa Rica: Neutrality, Militarism, and Resistance," Central American Case Study #6 leaflet (New York: War Resisters League, 1988), p. 2.
2. Although Costa Rica abolished its military in 1948, it retained a police force that assumes many of the duties of the former military. Consequently, Costa Rica is not entirely free of its reliance on militarism or conventional force.
3. Barash, *Introduction to Peace Studies,* p. 151.
4. James, "The Moral Equivalent of War," reprinted in Holmes, ed., *Nonviolence in America,* p. 147.

5. Quoted in Larry Lack, "Peace Brigades International," *The Whole Faith Review* (Spring 1990), p. 133.

6. Gene Sharp, *National Security Through Civilian-Based Defense* (Omaha, Nebr.: Association for Transarmament Studies, 1985), p. 24.

7. Quoted in *Victories Without Violence,* compiled by A. Ruth Fry (Santa Fe, N. Mex.: Ocean Tree Books, 1986), p. 26.

8. Alvin M. Josephy Jr. *Now That the Buffalo's Gone* (New York: Alfred A. Knopf, 1982), p. 229.

9. Norman Charles Freund, "Nonviolent National Defense" (Ph.D. diss., Southern Illinois University, 1980), pp. 60–76. See also Sharp, *National Security,* p. 28.

CHAPTER **14** Against All Odds

1. For a more detailed look at Gallaudet's protests, see Joseph Shapiro, *No Pity* (New York: Random House, 1993), chapter 3.

2. Quoted in David R. Weber, ed., *Civil Disobedience in America* (Ithaca, N.Y.: Cornell University Press, 1978), p. 32.

3. Quoted in Colman McCarthy, "War, Property and Peace," *Alternatives to Violence Reader,* p. 95.

Glossary

activist: a person who actively works for social or political change

ahimsa: Eastern concept of nonviolence

boycott: social, economic, or political noncooperation

civil disobedience: to break the law for a moral purpose

civil rights: legally guaranteed rights of all citizens

civilian-based defense: a government policy in which civilians are trained to use nonviolent resistance as a means of national defense

conscientious objection: to refuse to serve in the military for moral or religious reasons

direct action: violent or nonviolent protest that goes beyond the bounds of "normal" or routine political activity. Methods of nonviolent action, such as strikes, boycotts, and demonstrations, are all forms of direct action.

dissident: a person who actively disagrees and takes a public stand about his or her disagreement

embargo: an economic boycott initiated by a government against another nation

fast: to voluntarily go without food

genocide: systematic mass murder of an entire group of people because of their race, culture, or politics

noncooperation: the refusal to obey commands or laws or to participate, as a form of protest

nonresistance: the refusal to retaliate against violence by using violence

nonviolence: (1) to refrain from a violent act; or (2) to reject all violence for moral reasons

nonviolent conflict: a conflict in which at least one side commits to using nonviolent methods to wage the conflict

nonviolent discipline: to maintain nonviolent behavior regardless of how an opponent behaves

nonviolent methods: the "weapons" used in nonviolent conflict

nonviolent resistance: nonviolent struggle, usually through noncooperation with one's opponent

nonviolent sanctions: method of nonviolent action that causes one's opponent to suffer. For example, an economic boycott causes the opponent to lose money.

nonviolent strategy: the overall plan that activists use to make sure that all their resources and actions can work best, in order to bring about their goals and objectives

nonviolent struggle: when a person or group uses nonviolent methods to resolve a conflict or to protect themselves from harm

pacifism: the belief that violence is never morally justifiable in a struggle between nations; some people extend this commitment to personal interactions as well.

passive resistance: an older, inadequate term for noncooperation or nonviolent action. It fell out of popular usage because it was confused with passivity (doing nothing).

people power: the capacity of people to use nonviolent methods in conflict or defense; also refers to grassroots movements

petition: collective signatures to register a protest or solidarity

picket: a protest line, where people carry protest banners and verbalize their grievances to the public or to their opponent

pragmatic or **practical nonviolence:** nonviolence that is based on practical reasons

principled nonviolence: nonviolence based on religious faith or philosophical and moral reasoning

protest demonstration: when people publicly congregate in order to express a particular viewpoint

reconciliation: to resolve a conflict in a way that is beneficial to both parties

sanction: an act that imposes a cost on a person or group in an effort to change their behavior

satyagraha: the word coined for Mohandas Gandhi's theory of nonviolence; means "truth-force"

sit-in: refusal to leave premises as a form of protest

social action: to work to improve an injustice or solve a problem of society

strike: to refuse to work or go to school as a form of protest

tax resistance: to refuse to pay taxes as a form of protest, not merely to evade them for selfish reasons

vigil: nonviolent watch or silent demonstration

violence: force or the threat of force to injure or kill someone; also verbal assault and institutionalized forms of injustice, such as racism, poverty, and political oppression

Selected
Bibliography

Ackerman, Peter, and Kruegler, Christopher. *Strategic Nonviolent Conflict.*
   New York: Praeger, 1994.

Brown, Michael, and May, John. *The Greenpeace Story.* New York: Dorling
   Kindersley, 1991.

Cooney, Robert, and Michalowski, Helen, eds. *The Power of the People.*
   Philadelphia: New Society Publishers, 1987.

Gandhi, Mohandas. *An Autobiography: The Story of My Experiments with
   Truth.* Boston: Beacon Press, 1933.

Gregg, Richard B. *The Power of Non-violence.* New York: Schocken Books,
   1966.

Hall, Robert T. *The Morality of Civil Disobedience.* New York: Harper &
   Row, 1971.

Hedemann, Ed, ed. *War Resisters League Organizer's Manual.* New York:
   War Resisters League, 1986.

———. *War Tax Resistance.* 4th ed. Philadelphia: New Society Publishers,
   1992.

Herngren, Per. *Path of Resistance: The Practice of Civil Disobedience.*
   Translated by Margaret Rainey. Philadelphia: New Society Publishers,
   1993.

Selected Bibliography

Hunter, Doris, and Mallick, Krishna, eds. *Nonviolence: A Reader*. New York: University Press of America, 1990.

Juergensmeyer, Mark. *Fighting Fair: A Nonviolent Strategy for Resolving Everyday Conflicts*. New York: Harper & Row, 1986.

King Jr., Martin Luther. *Strength to Love*. Philadelphia: Fortress Press, 1963.

Lynd, Staughton, ed. *Nonviolence in America*. New York: The Bobbs-Merrill Co., 1966.

McAllister, Pam. *This River of Courage: Generations of Women's Resistance and Action*. Philadelphia: New Society, 1991.

———. *"You Can't Kill the Spirit": Stories of Women and Nonviolent Action*. Philadelphia: New Society Publishers, 1988.

Meltzer, Milton. *Ain't Gonna Study War No More*. New York: Harper & Row, 1985.

Seeley, Robert A. *The Handbook of Nonviolence*. Westport, Conn.: Lawrence Hill & Co., 1986.

Sharp, Gene. *The Role of Power in Nonviolent Struggle*. Volumes 1–3. Boston: Porter Sargent Publishers, 1973.

Shirer, William L. *Gandhi, A Memoir*. New York: Simon & Schuster, 1979.

Tolstoy, Leo. *Writings on Civil Disobedience and Nonviolence*. Philadelphia: New Society Publishers, 1987.

Vanderhaar, Gerard A. *Active Nonviolence—A Way of Personal Peace*. Mystic, Conn.: Twenty-Third, 1990.

Weber, David R., ed. *Civil Disobedience in America: A Documentary History*. Ithaca, N.Y.: Cornell University Press, 1978.

Wilcox, Fred A. *Uncommon Martyrs*. New York: Addison-Wesley, 1991.

Index

Page numbers in *italics* refer to photographs.

7/8/96